Pocket
Guide to
San
Francisco

FODOR'S TRAVEL PUBLICATIONS

are compiled, researched, and edited by an international team of travel writers, field correspondents, and editors. The series, which now almost covers the globe, was founded by Eugene Fodor in 1936.

OFFICES
New York & London

Fodor's Pocket San Francisco

Editors: Kathy Ewald, David Low
Maps and Plans: Pictograph
Illustrations: Ted Burwell
Cover Photograph: Mark Stephenson/West Light

Cover Design: Vignelli Associates

Fodor's 89

Pocket Guide to San Francisco

Carol Barrington

FODOR'S TRAVEL PUBLICATIONS, INC.
New York & London

Contents

Overview

This isn't a big city in the sprawling Los Angeles or high-density New York sense of the word—just slightly more than 700,000 souls neatly tucked into 46.6 unexpandable miles—and rooms at the most enjoyable hotels are at a premium almost year-round. Weekend reservations require six to twelve weeks advance notice, particularly in summer. Your next-best bet is calling at the very last moment in hope of picking up a cancellation.

THE CITY SIMPLIFIED

Twin Peaks provides San Francisco's most extensive panorama. These low hills top a residential district almost at the city's midpoint, and the view is prime. San Francisco Bay itself becomes a backdrop for a city that looks like a child's creation. At night the scene is an incredible mantle of lights.

2

OVERVIEW

Points of Interest

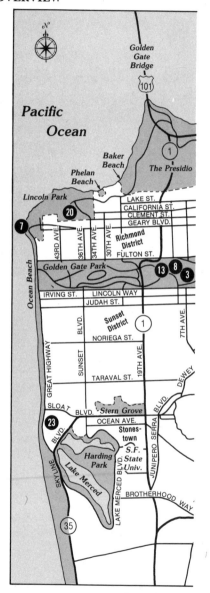

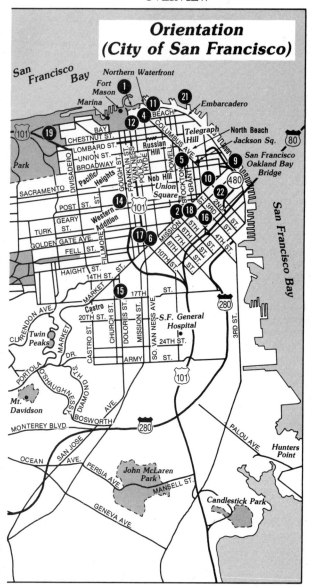

Orientation
(City of San Francisco)

Face north, and scan from east to west, right to left, Bay Bridge to the Golden Gate. Yerba Buena (Treasure Island) and the East Bay Hills are the dominant features to the east. Marin County, the gateway to both the Mendocino Coast and the wine country, is on the north. Behind you, to the south, are the San Francisco peninsula and San Jose.

The Bay Bridge angles off to the northeast, its San Francisco link a study in suspended but sturdy grace, its Oakland section a utilitarian mass of steel. Quite appropriate, some San Franciscans think!

The Castro and Mission districts, as well as the city's industrial heart, begin near the base of Twin Peaks and spread to the east. The slot—Market Street—angles northeast, dividing the Mission District from the spires of Civic Center and Downtown. The Fairmont, with its distinctive tower, marks Nob Hill, and from this distance Coit Tower seems the Fairmont's near neighbor, although Chinatown and North Beach nestle between the two. Much of the Embarcadero and Fisherman's Wharf area is out of sight in the center of your view, hidden behind Russian Hill.

To the north, the Golden Gate Bridge links San Francisco with Marin County. The large green zone at the south end of the bridge is the Presidio, so named by the Spanish in 1776 and still headquarters for the Sixth Army. Formerly closed, the Presidio now welcomes visitors as part of the Golden Gate National Recreation Area (GGNRA).

The hills of homes to the right of the Presidio, almost directly in the center of your bridge-to-bridge panorama, mark tony Pacific Heights and its neighbor, Cow Hollow (Union Street). The compact Marina District is north of Pacific Heights, edging the bay. Japantown, the Western Addition, and the Haight-Ashbury District roll south from Pacific Heights to the foot of Twin Peaks, in that order.

The second large and long patch of green south of the Presidio and to your left is the Golden Gate Park. North of the park is the Richmond District, and to the south is the Sunset District, both of which have things of interest to tourists.

Twin Peaks is easily reached by car, one of the prime stops on the highly recommended 49-Mile Drive. Special blue-and-white seagull signs mark this scenic circuit that begins at Civic Center.

If you haven't a car, numerous firms offer tours of Twin Peaks and the 49-Mile Drive, as well as of the greater Bay Area. A complete list is available from the San Francisco Convention & Visitors Bureau (see end of the general information chapter). City tours cost $15–$25. Specialty walking tours of the city's cafés, neighborhoods, discount shops, art galleries, jazz clubs, and photo sites also are listed.

Don't miss two other outstanding views of the city. Coit Tower on Telegraph Hill lies downtown with the waterfront at your feet; the elevator (cost, $1) to the top of the tower operates from 11 A.M. to 4:15 P.M. daily. In all, San Francisco has ten skyrooms, the best of which is the Carnelian Room, 779 feet above the 500 block of California Street on the 52d floor of the Bank of America building.

THE NEIGHBORHOODS

Touring San Francisco is best done by districts. Although the most enjoyable shops, hotels, and restaurants will be discussed in detail in following sections, here are the best things to see in each area.

Downtown sightseeing usually begins at or near Union Square, an open plaza surrounded for blocks by the best of hotels, shopping, and restaurants. The noted I. Magnin store plus Saks, Neimans, Macy's, and countless specialty shops are here. Two cable car lines turn and load at the foot of Powell Street (at Market), and the Tourist Information Center is on the lower level of the adjacent Hallidie Plaza, as are the Bay Area Rapid Transit (BART) and Muni Metro subway stations. You can ride the cable cars up Powell to Nob Hill and transfer to the California Street line headed down to the Financial District. There you'll find the four towers of Embarcadero Center for shopping, dining, and strolling, and the Ferry Building, which is the terminal for trips to Sausalito and Larkspur. From there, Market Street leads uptown to Civic Center, home to the city's noted symphony, ballet, and opera companies, and then on to the Castro district.

The ornate China Gate on Grant Avenue (at Sutter) in downtown marks the beginning of tourist **Chinatown,** but Stockton Street, one block west, is the true heart of the largest Chinese community outside Asia. A turn east on Washington or Jackson streets brings you to **Jackson Square** and all that remains of the old Barbary coast, which is now a historic district. The brick warehouses have been refurbished into offices and decorator to-the-trade showrooms, but a few trendy shops and watering holes fill in around the edges.

From here, Columbus Avenue angles northwest, the main drag of **North Beach.** This is San Francisco's Italian heart, home to espresso, sidewalk cafés, sourdough bakeries, boccie ball, pasta factories, and the most colorful night action in the city. Upper Grant is a micro-neighborhood of its own, and Coit Tower surveys all from nearby Telegraph Hill.

The **Northern Waterfront** stretches from the Presidio to the Ferry Building and includes Fort Point, the Marina, Fort Mason and Aquatic Park, Fisherman's Wharf, Ghirardelli Square, the Cannery, and Pier 39. Bay boat trips leave from piers 39, 41, and 43½.

Union Street is boutique, restaurant, and gallery row, a series of upscale blocks west of Van Ness in **Pacific Heights.** You can tour several Victorian mansions here and also shop on interesting, less sleek Sacramento Street.

Japantown is west of downtown via either Geary or Sutter. Small and compact, it has many excellent Japanese restaurants, sushi bars, and stores, and one open shopping area is patterned after a small Japanese village. **Golden Gate Park** is worth a full day, site of both the Asian Art and de Young museums, the Academy of Natural Sciences (which includes Morrison Planetarium and Steinhart Aquarium), the Japanese Tea Garden, and Strybing Arboretum. The **Richmond District**, with Clement Street's restaurants, lies to the north of the park. The **Haight-Ashbury District** parallels the park's panhandle with several blocks of interesting shops and eateries, and the **Great Highway** at the western end of the park edges Ocean Beach. Now part of the Golden Gate National Recreation Area, this strip of shore includes Cliff House and Seal Rocks, the Palace of the Legion of Honor, Fort Funston, and the San Francisco Zoo.

After surveying San Francisco's highlights on a tour, you'll want to return to your favorites for a closer look on foot. But you need not explore alone. Volunteer city guides give free tours (donations appreciated) in many areas on specific days. Call 558–3981 for current information. Areas usually covered include City Hall, Coit Tower, Pacific Heights, Cathedral

Hill/Japantown, Cow Hollow (Union Street), Nob Hill, Market Street, North Beach, and the Golden Gate Bridge. A similar free guide program tours parts of Golden Gate Park (221–1311) on weekends, May through October.

How about a tour through the city's ethnic markets, or an insider's look at Chinatown? These walks and other explorations on foot are offered for a fee by several firms. Ask the San Francisco Convention & Visitors Bureau for details.

In recent years Castro Street, south of Market to 19th Street, has become an internationally known haven for homosexuals and something of a tourist attraction. Two other primarily gay areas are less benign: **Polk Street** between Washington and Geary, and **Folsum Street.** Also be aware that the **Western Addition** and **Fillmore District** have high crime rates; use caution.

General Information

San Francisco is blessed with the world's most magnificent site, and therein lies a major clue to its enduring charm. Surrounded on three sides by water, the city enjoys a springlike climate almost year-round. With the exception of a few September and October days in the high 80s, you'll find temperatures in the 60s during summer, 50–57 degrees in winter, with acceptable humidity. Readings on either side of the 45–75 degree range bring on headlines, and the most measurable snow—3.7 inches—fell in February 1887!

Whenever you come, bring a coat and umbrella. You'll need a wrap at night in every season, even summer. Sweaters and a lightweight windbreaker also come in handy.

Although temperatures are mild, expect some wet and gloomy days December through mid-March. Up to four inches of rain falls in each of those months, usually not in torrents but slowly over extended periods. Activities move indoors with multiple New Year's celebrations in the Civic Center area and two boat-sport shows in January. You'll also find the performing arts in full season at the Louise M. Davies Symphony Hall and the War Memorial Opera House in Civic Center as well as in the downtown theatre district near Union Square. The Chinese New Year Celebration in February is San Francisco at its unique best.

Winter is also a grand time to visit Yosemite, 200 miles east. The crowds are elsewhere, and the valley in snow is pristine grandeur. A call to (209) 372–0264 accesses information on snow conditions, backcountry campsites, roads, and weather. The skiing and social activity are better, however, farther north in the Lake Tahoe region, particularly at Heavenly Valley, overlooking the lake, and at Squaw Valley, site of the 1960 Winter Olympics. A third resort, Alpine Meadows, is a tradition with San Francisco families.

Crisp and clearing spring kicks off with a big St. Patrick's Day celebration in mid-March, followed by the Cherry Blossom Festival in late April, the most elaborate Japanese cultural event outside Nippon. The cherry trees in the Japanese Tea Garden and giant beds of rhododendrons in the city's parks bloom well into April.

May brings the zany Bay-to-Breakers footrace across town, and June through August spotlight the arts. Special performances by the opera, ballet, symphony, and other arts groups highlight the San Francisco Summer Festival, and summer Sundays mean afternoon concerts at Stern Grove.

Although San Francisco is the nation's fourth sunniest city, morning and evening fogs are part of the city's unique mystique and are most common in summer. Often, the first sound you'll hear in the pre-dawn morning is what local sage and columnist Herb Caen calls the "Fugue of Five Fog Horns," and some natives swear they can identify each horn by its own distinctive sound.

Watching the fog roll through the Golden Gate to blanket the city and its bay is a not-to-be-missed experience. If you've hit a streak of sunshine, don't worry. All it takes is two or three days of warm temperatures to throw the fog switch. From June through September the summer sun usually burns through around 10 A.M. and disappears in gray mist by mid-afternoon. At other times, Nob Hill and Twin Peaks may be basking in sunshine while Market Street, the Embarcadero, and the western beach remain wrapped in fog—or vice versa.

Being predictable equates with boring, and San Francisco is neither.

But it can be a bit smug. Blessed with natural air-conditioning much of the year, the city doesn't bother much with the artificial kind. You'll find this a disadvantage during the almost-annual heat wave of late September/early October, when you'll want your hotel room windows open for ventilation. The street noise winds down after midnight, and the garbage trucks rev up between 4 and 5 A.M. Your best defenses are to use ear plugs, stay in one of the newer, air-conditioned hotels, or to request a quiet room as far away from the street as possible.

WHAT TO PACK

Year-round, San Francisco is a grand sweater-and-slacks town for both men and women, but that's about as casual as things get. Although the city's hat-and-gloves days for the ladies are long gone, San Franciscans still dress with pride and style, and it's fun to play that game while you're here. Dressing well is definitely part of this city's cosmopolitan scene, whether it's the latest in Euro-design or a well-cut classic.

Jogging clothes are used for jogging or running, not for street wear, and while men can get away with clean chinos and a sport shirt for daytime sightseeing, slacks and a sport coat should be worn in the better restaurants at lunch, a coat and tie at dinner.

For sightseeing, women will be comfortable in well-tailored pant suits or blazer/slacks combinations; dresses, often with a jacket; and blouse/skirt ensembles. Pack something chic or high-fashioned for at least one grand night out, and don't forget some sort of evening wrap and bag.

The tourist circuit—Golden Gate Park/Chinatown/North Beach/Fisherman's Wharf—is the only exception to the above, and that's because visitors often outnumber the natives in those areas. However, even here you'll see message T-shirts, halter tops, short shorts, etc., only on those who don't care and on the very young. Jeans and cool cottons (always take a sweater!) are better choices. Save your more casual wear for a ferry outing to Angel Island, Alcatraz, Tiburon, or Larkspur.

This is a walker's town, so you'll need comfortable walking shoes, preferably with cushioned soles. Ladies, save your high heels for evening; they won't cope with San Francisco's hills. Also pack a lightweight tote with comfortable shoulder or back straps for carrying guide books, maps, and picnics while you are here and for packing your souvenirs when it's time to go.

TRIP TIPS

If you arrive by air, you will land at San Francisco International Airport in San Bruno on the peninsula, 14 miles and 20–30 minutes south of downtown. Transportation between the airport and San Francisco is by cab (about $25); SFO Airporter bus to Fisherman's Wharf and one downtown terminal ($6; 673–2433); and several other transfer services that provide door-to-door service throughout the bay area ($6–$8 by advance reservation). For further details, call the Visitors Bureau at 974–6900 for general information on getting into the city.

Although you can pick up a rental car at the airport, it is neither advisable nor necessary. Parking is limited and expensive in many parts of the city, and you can easily get around as many San Franciscans do, by a combination of bus, cab, or cable car. Should you want a rental car for special explorations or out-of-town trips, you'll find a score of agencies within blocks of Union Square and at many of the major hotels.

Some cost-cutting hints (all the more to spend at I. Magnin's or Top of the Mark!): Comparison-shop for rental rates by telephone, and make car reservations before leaving home if possible; the lower-cost compacts with automatic transmissions (best for coping with vertical SF) are in short supply from June through October. Use a credit card to rent the car; otherwise you may have to leave a hefty cash deposit that can devastate your trip budget. Once you are in town, check for discount car rental ads in the many tourist publications you'll find around the city; latest quotes go as low as $19.95 a day with free mileage, pickup, and delivery (read the fine print, however). Generally, the three- and five-day unlimited mileage rates are the lowest, so consider combining your arrival or departure with a day trip out of the city. Ask if you can pick up a car at the airport and return it in the city, or vice versa.

Street parking is possible throughout the city, but read the posted signs carefully. Each street has a different cleaning day (or night), time limit, or other restriction that can result in an improperly parked car being promptly towed away. When making your hotel reservation, ask about parking availability and fees. You may be better off shopping around for a garage. Some have weekly rates in the $40–$50 range, and almost all post rates in a confusing manner. Be sure you understand, or you may find that that $1.50 deal was per half hour! Two of the best bets downtown are the Stockton-Sutter Garage, on Sutter between Stockton and Grant; and the Downtown Center Garage at the corner of Mason and O'Farrell.

Amtrak serves San Francisco daily, from Denver, Seattle, Los Angeles, San Jose, Portland, San Diego, Chicago, and the San Joaquin Valley. The rail service terminates in Oakland, but the ticket price includes charter bus transfer to the Trans-Bay Bus Terminal, First and Mission streets, in San Francisco. For information, call 415–982–8512 (or 800–USA–RAIL).

Green Tortoise (821–0803), Greyhound Bus Lines (433–1500), and Trailways Bus System (982–6400) have bus service to San Francisco from various parts of the country. If out of town, call your local bus office for information.

Automobile access to San Francisco can be either swift and efficient (U.S. 101 and Interstates 80 and 280) or a driving experience you'll remember all your life (State Highway 1).

U.S. 101 is, for the most part, a divided multilane highway that links the city to San Mateo and Santa Clara counties to the south and, via the Golden Gate Bridge, to Marin and Sonoma counties to the north. Interstate 80 crosses the Bay Bridge to Oakland, Sacramento, Tahoe, and points east, and Interstate 280 rolls south to San Jose on a handsome route through the hills of the San Francisco peninsula.

State Highway 1, on the other hand, is an only-in-California adventure for the strong of hand and heart—a narrow two-lane road that hugs and twists along much of the coast from the Mexican border to the Oregon state line.

Do note that pedestrians have the right-of-way in California and will expect you to stop for them, particularly if they are in the crosswalk. Also, when you park on any of San Francisco's hills, cant your front wheels into the curb—it's the law.

TIPS FOR BRITISH VISITORS

British visitors to San Francisco will need a valid 10-year passport (cost: £15) and a U.S. Visitor's Visa. Visas are obtainable through travel agents or by post from the *U.S. Embassy,* Visa and Immigration Dept., 5 Upper Grosvenor St., London W1A 2JB (tel. 01/499–3443).

It is a good idea to insure yourself to cover health, loss of luggage (though check that this isn't already covered in any existing homeowner's policies you may have), trip cancellation, and motoring mishaps while you are in San Francisco. *Europ Assistance,* 252 High St., Croydon, Surrey CRO 1NF (tel. 01/680–1234) offers excellent service.

Tour operators offering packages to San Francisco include: *Jetways,* 93 Newman St., London W1P 3LE (tel. 01/637–5444). Jetways will create a whole package—choose from flights from £469, hotels from £21.25 to £36 per person, per night, sharing a double room, and there's also the bonus of free car rental between November and March. *Jetsave,* Sussex House, London Rd., East Grinstead, West Sussex RH19 1LD (tel. 0342/316123) offers hotel vacations in San Francisco with prices from £599 to £709 per person, with options on car rental from £72 per week. *Page & Moy,* 136–140 London Rd., Leicester LE2 1EN (tel. 0533/552996) offers three-city vacations in Las Vegas, Los Angeles, and San Francisco, with five of the 14 nights in San Francisco. Prices from £749 to £849 per person, sharing a double room; meals not included. *Poundstretcher,* Airlink House, Hazlewick Ave., Three Bridges, Crawley, West Sussex RH10 1YS (tel. 0293/518022) offers two-center vacations, with seven nights in San Francisco and seven in Los Angeles. Prices from £825 to £1,199 per person; meals not included. *Premier Holidays,* Premier Travel Center, Westbrook, Milton Rd., Cambridge CB4 1YQ (tel. 0223/355977) offers seven-day packages in San Francisco, from £585 in budget-grade hotels to £1,345 in superior-grade hotels. Prices are for accommodations only but include free car rental.

The best bet for low-cost air tickets if you're traveling independently is to get an APEX ticket from any of the major air lines serving the U.S.A., among them American Airlines, tel. 01/834–5151; British Airways, tel. 01/897–4000; Continental Airlines, tel. 0293/776–4646; Delta Airlines, tel. 01/668–0935; Pan Am, tel. 01/409–3377; Virgin Atlantic Airways, tel. 0293/38222. APEX tickets cost from about £469. Another good source of bargain-priced fares is in the small ads of daily or Sunday newspapers. Prices here are from £350 but check if airport taxes are included in the price quoted.

Returning to Britain, you may bring home: (1) 200 cigarettes or 100 cigarillos or 50 cigars or 250 grams of tobacco; (2) two liters of table wine and, in addition, (a) one liter of alcohol over 22% by volume (most spirits), (b) two liters of alcohol under 22% by volume (fortified or sparkling wine), or (c) two liters of table wine; (3) 50 grams of perfume and 1/4 liter of toilet water; and (4) other goods up to a value of £32.

For free information on San Francisco and for advice on your trip, contact the United States Travel and Tourism Administration, 22 Sackville St., London W1X 2EA (tel. 01/439–7433).

IN-TOWN TOURING

Getting around San Francisco without a car is easy, thanks to Muni. The Municipal Railway System covers much of town with motor or trolley buses, shoppers' shuttles, street cars, and a new, but limited, subway. Easy-to-read Muni maps are $1.25 at City Hall, book and drugstores, hotels, and metro stations citywide, or you can call 673–MUNI for information. The fare is 75 cents in exact change, and transfers allow further Muni travel for up to 90 minutes. All-day Muni passes ($5) also are available.

The city's cable cars are back on their three routes, ready for a second charming century after a $60-million rejuvenation of the entire system. The fare is $1.50, or 75 cents with a valid Muni transfer.

Although numerous firms offer tours of the city, touring by tape is fun. You'll find a variety of cassettes on sale at many bookstores, including *Books, Inc.,* 140 Powell; and *Book Passage,* 57 Post, 4th Floor. Want to pet a tiger? Explore a sewer? Go behind the scenes at an aquarium? Pick up a few tapes from *Near Escapes,* Box 3005, San Francisco 94119 (921–1392).

NICE TO KNOW

San Francisco is in the Pacific time zone, three hours behind Eastern time. The telephone area code is 415, information is 411, and in case of emergency you can get help by dialing 911 from any telephone without charge. For information on the day's events, call 391–2001, or stop by one of the numerous Teleguide terminals scattered around town, a free electronic public information service.

Additional information sources include the San Francisco Convention and Visitors Bureau, Box 6977, San Francisco, CA 94101 (974–6900), and the Redwood Empire Association, One Market Plaza, Spear Street Tower, Suite 1001, San Francisco, CA 94105 (543–8334).

San Francisco's current sales tax is 6.5 percent; the hotel tax is 11 percent.

Downtown

Most of the best reasons for visiting San Francisco are con-
centrated here in three distinct areas: Union Square/Nob
Hill, the Embarcadero Center/Financial District, and Civic
Center. Many of the finest hotels, the most elegant restaurants, outstanding entertainments, the best shopping—all lie
northwest of the two-mile stretch of Market Street between
the Ferry Building and Van Ness Avenue. For tourists, it's
a bonanza. To most San Franciscans, it is the focus of their
world.

Union Square is the hub of San Francisco. While you can
walk to either Civic Center or Embarcadero Center, it's best
to save your feet and energy and ride the bus or Muni Metro
subway. A "How to Get There From Union Square" information sheet covers all of San Francisco, available from the
Redwood Empire Visitor Information Center.

UNION SQUARE

Boxed by Powell, Post, Stockton, and Geary streets, Union Square is home to pigeons, panhandlers, prophets, and patricians. Noontime orators hold forth while office workers picnic and well-dressed shoppers sashay between Neiman's, Magnin's, and Saks.

Shopping

With its uniformed, limousine-whistling doorman, **I. Magnin & Co.** could be intimidating if it wasn't so much fun. Music often serenades the sidewalk from tiny speakers above the store's windows, and Narsai's Cafe on the lower level serves daily specials like Chinese Duck Salad or Chicken Breast Circassian with a glass of the appropriate wine at reasonable cost.

In Magnin's you can sample six of the world's classic perfumes from an array of antique Baccarat crystal decanters at the glittering Caron boutique on the ground floor—a quarter ounce in a tiny Baccarat crystal bottle is $40, but sniffing is free!—or finding dreamy designer clothes on sale in the main aisles of upstairs fashion floors. AE/DC/MC/V/ Magnin credit cards.

Next door is **Macy's,** not as extensive as its New York counterpart, but close. In spring the store blooms with its annual flower show, a visual extension of the rhododendrons that color Union Square across the street. Don't miss the basement housewares department, one of the most imaginative and extensive collections of domestic gadgets in the country. There is also a post office hidden in the back of the basement.

For generations, a San Francisco shopping tradition called the City of Paris shared the Stockton and Geary intersection with I. Magnin's, its handsome rotunda topped with a stained-glass replica of Sir Francis Drake's ship, the *Golden Hind.* Today, this is the gleaming **Neiman-Marcus,** and that ship sails above the **Rotunda Restaurant,** an elegant cream-and-gold setting for lunch or a late-afternoon treat. From 3 to 5 P.M., it's petite tea Monday through Saturday, high tea Thursday through Saturday, and the setting couldn't be bet-

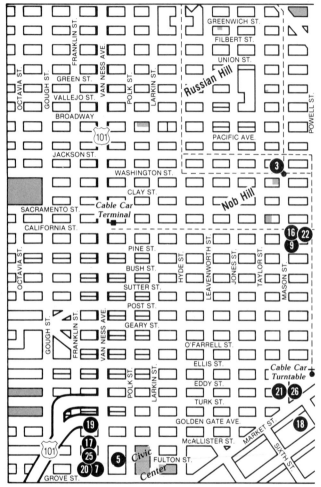

Points of Interest

1) Bank of America Building
2) Bank of California
3) Cable Car Barn & Museum
4) Campton Place Hotel
5) City Hall
6) Coit Tower

7) Davies Symphony Hall
8) Embarcadero Center
9) Fairmont Hotel
10) Ferry Building
    (World Trade Center)
11) Golden Gateway Center
12) Hyatt Regency Hotel
13) John's Grill

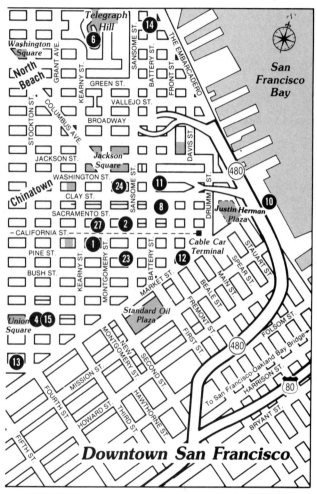

14) Levi Plaza
15) Maidep Lane
16) Mark Hopkins-Intercontinental Hotel
17) Museum of Modern Art
18) Old U.S. Mint
19) Opera Center Development
20) Opera House
21) Ramada Renaissance Hotel
22) Stanford Court
23) Stock Exchange
24) Transamerica Pyramid
25) Veteran's Building
26) Visitor Information Center
27) Wells Fargo Bank

ter. There are fresh flowers on the tables, and the passing parade of Union Square is visible through the large windows. One thing nice to know before you order everything in sight: only AE, Neiman charge cards, and cash are accepted.

One of the best things about the Union Square area is shopping in **Maiden Lane**—No. 140 is the only Frank Lloyd Wright-designed building in San Francisco—and at **Gump's,** 250 Post St. (982–1616). The latter is a San Francisco institution, founded by Solomon Gump in 1861 as a frame and molding shop. Today, Gump's is known worldwide for its collections of Oriental jade and antiques, unique precious jewelry, and the best in silver, fine china, and crystal. Even though there now are branches of Gump's elsewhere, none comes even close to the original.

Walking through the main floor is akin to browsing in a comfortable museum, but you can buy these lovely things—often at a surprisingly affordable price. The store motto is "Good taste costs no more," but aside from sales and special purchase items, you shouldn't expect discounts. The jade and Imari collections are dear enough to be under lock and key, and Baccarat, Lalique, *et al.* have their own special niches of pricey elegance. Also here: unusual designer clothing, heirloom quality gifts, handsome one-of-a-kind furniture, and the finest of stationeries. Closed on Sunday.

Hotels

If cost is absolutely no deterrent, and you want to be pampered beyond belief, reserve a room at the new **Portman.** Every room comes with a personal valet who will whisk your clothes off for pressing, draw your bath, clean shoes you leave lying about, etc. The personal service is the best in the city. Except for tips, all is included in the $185–$285 single, $220–$320 double price, but weekend packages can cut those costs considerably. 500 Post St., San Francisco, CA 94102; 415–771–8600 or 800–533–6465.

Should you prefer to have San Francisco at your feet, however, consider the 36-story **Hyatt on Union Square.** Each of its 693 rooms has a full-length glass door that slides open, giving guests the sensation of being poised for flight above downtown. Regular rooms are $218 single, $248 double; Regency Club rooms are $238 single, $268 double. Generally, the higher the room, the higher the rate. Pluses include free early-morning limo service to the Embarcadero for jogging or to the Financial District. (345 Stockton St., San Francisco 94108; 415–398–1234 or 800–228–9000.)

Campton Place Hotel, across from the Hyatt on Stockton Street, is an only-in-San-Francisco experience. Small, posh, and emphasizing personal service, Campton Place has individually furnished rooms with the cushiest of designer bedspreads, deep carpets, fine-quality furniture, fresh flowers, and limited-edition art. A maid will unpack your bags when you arrive, and pack them up again (with swan-logo tissue) when you depart. Rates are $180–$250, single or double. (340 Stockton St., San Francisco 94108; 415–781–5555; in CA: 800–235–4300; elsewhere: 800–647–4007.)

Nothing could be more San Francisco than the main entrance to the new $125-million **Ramada Renaissance Hotel,** our fourth luxury choice. Seven tall, sculptured panels by local artist Ruth Asawa depict the city's distinctive neighborhoods and citizenry, from Father Serra to Joe Montana. Another $1 million in artwork is scattered around the public areas of this 1,004-room beauty. The hotel is aptly named. Its construction has brought a wave of gentrification to the area. Special here: full concierge service on the top four floors, plus a Clark Hatch Physical Fitness Center. Rooms range from $125–$185, single or double. (55 Cyril Magnin, Market St. at Fifth St., San Francisco 94102; 415–392–8000 or 800–228–9898.)

The following hotels are affordable downtown finds. Each is handsomely decorated and has one of the city's most notable restaurants on the premises as an additional drawing card. When reserving, ask specifically about air-conditioning, in-room refrigerators, valet parking, complimentary limo service within the downtown area, and wine and cheese parties.

The **Galleria Park Hotel** is adjacent to the classy shops of the Galleria at Crocker Center and has both a garden and a running track on the roof. One of the city's best fish houses, Bentley's, opens onto the lobby. Rooms are $110, single or double; suites are $135–$350. (191 Sutter St., San Francisco 94104; 415–781–3060; 800–792–9855 in CA; 800–792–9639 in U.S.)

The **Juliana Hotel** is a decorator's dream of mirrored walls, pastel carpets, and swagged drapes over Roman shades. The famed Palm Restaurant, with its cartoons of SF's mega-people, is just off the lobby. Rooms are $94; suites are $115–$125. (590 Bush St., San Francisco 94108; 415–392–2540; 800–372–8800 in CA; 800–382–8800 in U.S.)

In 1984 the **Hotel Vintage Court** had the highest occupancy rate in America, so don't drop in without a reservation. Ditto at Masa's, one of the toniest restaurants in town. Rooms are $94. (650 Bush St., San Francisco 94108; 415–392–4666; 800–654–7266 in CA; 800–654–1100 in U.S.)

The rooms are contemporary and the lobby Italian at the new **Villa Florence,** a classy redo only steps from Union Square and on the Powell Street cable-car line. Its $700,000 Kuleto's restaurant (Italian) is one of the most popular and affordable in town. Rooms are $99; suites are $119–$169. (225 Powell St., San Francisco 94108; 415–397–7700; 800–243–5700 in CA; 800–553–4411 in U.S.)

If you love canopied beds and a Williamsburg atmosphere, the **Monticello Inn** is a fine choice. Just off Union Square, this 91-room hotel is paired (incongruously) with the Corona Bar and Grill, noted for its trendy Cal-Mex fare. Rooms (some nonsmoking) are $99; suites are $129–$149. (80 Cyril Magnin St., San Francisco 94102; 415–392–8800 or 800–669–7777.)

Ah, but you want something cozy and intimate, perhaps with breakfast at your beck and call? America's bed-and-breakfast craze has its own special style in San Francisco, and it's almost always a more charming and less expensive alternative to staying in a hotel. Some of the following downtown B&Bs are cozy inns tucked amid skyscrapers. Others are sleek, full-service hostelries, complete with restaurants and cabarets. All are outstanding accommodations that include either croissants and coffee or individual microwaves and refrigerators in their daily rates.

The **Hotel Diva** is unique, a contemporary Italian gem that features VCRs in every high-ceilinged bedroom. There's a 200-tape library on site as well as a personal computer (bring your own floppy disk). The peach-and-champagne-colored rooms have highly stylized lacquered furniture, stereo TV, down comforters on oversized beds, original art, and luxurious baths. A Continental breakfast comes with the $99–$109 room rate, and valet parking with in-and-out privileges is $16. Opera and theater packages are house specialties, and you'll find the signatures and handprints of assorted divas in the front sidewalk. Best of all, the staff is friendly and competent. (440 Geary St., San Francisco 94102; 415–885–0200 or 800–553–1900.)

A less expensive charmer, the **Hotel Union Square,** is tucked amid the somewhat seedy storefronts of the 100 block of Powell St. Yet its lobby is elegant Art Deco, the staff is young and energetic, and the 141 rooms are comfortable. Built in 1913, this hotel has sheltered generations of writers and theater folk, among them Dashiell Hammett and Lillian Hellman. Rooms are $82–$99 (request the quiet ones at the back), and suites and penthouses are $185–$350 (two have private sundecks). All have private baths. Parking ($14) is behind the hotel on Ellis St. (114 Powell St., San Francisco 94102; 415–397–3000 or 800–553–1900.

If you love the opera and symphony, make reservations far in advance at the tiny but elegant **Inn at the Opera** in Civic Center. The Continental breakfast carries an additional $4.50 charge, but each of the 48 rooms has both a microwave and a refrigerator, and the concierge can direct you to nearby bakeries. Visualize huge bouquets of fresh flowers on antique chests, Chinese vases in lighted niches, puffy comforters and banks of pillows on queen-size beds, and decorated bathrooms, and you will grasp the essence of this luxurious place. Rooms are $99–$130; suites are $140–$180. Check on holiday and weekend packages to lower those costs. Parking can be a problem. (333 Fulton St., San Francisco 94102; 415–863–8400; 800–423–9610 in CA; 800–325–2708 in U.S.)

Brass coach lamps mark the entrance to the **Inn at Union Square,** an elegant retreat tucked next to the very British Swaine Adeney shop on Post Street. Just half a block from Union Square, this seems another world, with its quiet library lobby and air of distinction. Each of the 30 rooms has its own brass door knocker and bath, and the decor runs to Georgian furniture and canopied beds. A lavish Continental breakfast and late afternoon tea are included, followed by hors d'oeuvres and sherry, and if you want a picnic, just ask the concierge. The entire atmosphere here is one of comfort and service, and the carriage-trade clientele loves it—this is their pied-à-terre in the city. Expect some Louis Vuitton luggage-types amid the Samsonite crowd. Daily rates are $95–$300 single; $105–$300 double. (440 Post St., San Francisco 94102; 415–397–3510.)

Although the **Kensington Park Hotel** looks and acts like a hotel, it is adding some deluxe touches to the bed-and-breakfast scene. Beautifully decorated rooms have marble, brass, and glass baths and the best of mattresses, decked out in quality linens. The breakfast croissants come from Bakers of Paris, and sherry and tea enliven the lobby from 4 to 6 P.M. daily. Theater on the Square is on the premises. Rates are $99 single or double. (450 Post St., San Francisco 94102; 415–788–6400 or 800–553–1900.)

The **Petite Auberge** is a tough place to get a reservation. The 26 rooms are cozy, with ruffled spreads and pillows, and many have fireplaces that blaze with a flick of a wall switch. The lower level also has a comfortable living room with fireplace, couches, etc., where wine and tea are served in the late afternoon. Guests mix and share discoveries—a binder holds a treasury of restaurant recommendations, complete with pithy comments—and often join forces for an evening on the town. You'll find lawyers and doctors here, along with newlyweds, journalists, teachers—a cross-section of the young spirit between the ages of 30 and 60-plus. Rooms are $105–$155. Splurge for the better rooms, preferably at the back. A très secluded suite is $195. (863 Bush St., San Francisco 94108; 415–928–6000.)

Billed as an English-garden retreat, the new 27-room **White Swann Inn** is the British cousin of its next-door neighbor, Petite Auberge. All the rooms have fireplaces, refrigerators, and private baths, and the price includes a bountiful breakfast just off the garden and, late in the day, English high tea in the library. Rooms are $145–$160; the one suite is $250. (845 Bush St., San Francisco 94108; 415–775–1755.)

Dining

For a trip back to old San Francisco, try **Sam's Grill,** 374 Bush St., at Belden (421–0594). Sam's has been serving some of the best fresh seafood in the city since 1867. Originally in the old California market, Sam's is now just downhill from the Chinatown gate, within easy walking distance of Union Square.

First-timers think they have stumbled into a funeral in the foyer. All the waiters and bartenders are in black, and the ever-present crowd of waiting businessmen wear the SF uniform, a dark suit. However, Sam's is far from formal, and casual dress is fine. The bar is in front of a plain vanilla room filled with folks devouring the likes of deviled crab à la Sam's, clams Elizabeth, or Sam's special seafood platter. The fried calamari steak à la Sam's also is recommended (calamari is squid, San Francisco's newest passion and an acquired taste). Aside from a few framed hunting scenes and a line of coat hooks marching the length of the room atop the wood wainscoting, don't expect "decor." A Tiffany-type lamp in Sam's would be as out of place as quiche. The dinner and lunch menus are identical, change daily, and range from $8 to $20. Open Monday through Friday, but no reservations are accepted. Arrive before 11:45 A.M. for lunch, before 6:15 P.M. for dinner to avoid the wait. MC/V.

While **Napper's Too** is part of the Hyatt on Union Square, 345 Stockton St., it fronts on a sunny, streetside plaza and seems to have an identity of its own. Food at this inexpensive cafeteria/deli/coffeehouse ranges from fresh soups, salads, and sandwiches to homemade desserts, ice cream, and sorbets. No hard liquor, but you won't notice thanks to the vast selection of beers, wines, cappuccino, and espressos. All can be packed to go for picnics at no extra cost; just call 398-1234. Open Monday through Saturday, 11 A.M. to 4:30 P.M. AE/CB/DC/MC/V.

China Moon at 639 Post St. is another only-in-SF place, an always crowded café noted for inventive California/Chinese dishes like cosmic chaos soup, baked Buddha's buns, and some of the most outstanding desserts in the city. Don't miss the "Dim Sum And Then Sum" lunch. Owner/chef Barbara Tropp uses all fresh ingredients, without even a pinch of MSG. Open Tuesday through Saturday for lunch and dinner; reservations strongly advised for the latter. (775-4789). AE/MC/V.

Campton Place is soft-peach elegant, with the best of crystal, china, and service, a beautiful showcase for the inventive talents of chef Bradley Ogden. Breakfasts are extraordinary, pricey, and worth every penny; so are the dinners. Imagine what pine-nut dressing does for roasted chicken, or ginger sauce and fried oysters to Missouri ham. The menu changes to reflect the best foods available. Open daily, and reservations are required. (Off the lobby of the Campton Place Hotel, 340 Stockton St.; 781–5555.) AE/CB/DC/MC/V.

More casual, affordable, and fun in another way is **John's Grill,** 63 Ellis St., between Stockton and Powell streets (986–DASH). The phone number refers to famed mystery writer Dashiell Hammett, who not only ate at John's in the 1920's (it opened in 1908) but also saw to it that his famous detective Sam Spade ". . . went to John's Grill, asked the waiter to hurry his order of chips, baked potato, sliced tomatoes . . ." in his mystery genre classic, *The Maltese Falcon.* There are Dash memorabilia and photos of old San Francisco around the wood-paneled walls, and the Maltese Falcon room and Hammett's Den upstairs are SF favorites for both lunch and dinner. Reservations are advised at all times. (474–8005). AE/MC/V.

Janot's, a small French brasserie at 44 Campton Place, is authentic enough to attract a steady stream of Europeans. The brick-and-brass atmosphere is unpretentious, the daily specials so delicious you may become a regular yourself. Chef Pierre Morin, who learned to cook in his native Loire Valley, particularly recommends the fish dishes—"They always are *very* fresh"—preceded by a *tortière* of eggplant, tomatoes, zucchini, and smoked salmon. The quail salad (grilled and boneless) and the *confit* of duck leg nestled in watercress are other favorites. Prices are moderate; reservations advised. Open Monday through Saturday, lunch and dinner. (392–5373). AE/MC/V.

Entertainment

Made your plans for the evening? If not, stop between 12 noon and 7:30 P.M. at **STBS** (San Francisco Ticket Box Office Service) on the Stockton Street side of Union Square (opposite Maiden Lane) and see which performing-arts tickets are going for half-price. Sales are for cash only on the day of the performance, and the ticket booth is closed on Sunday and Monday. A call to 433–STBS will give you recorded information.

Care to shadow Sam Spade through the streets of San Francisco? Just reread *The Maltese Falcon* and then sign up for Don Herron's **Dashiell Hammett Tour.** Herron greets you in a trench coat and snap-brim hat, à la Humphrey Bogart's portrayal of Spade in the movie classic, and the adventure begins. No reservations are necessary. Just bring $5 to the steps of the public library at Civic Center, Larkin and McAllister streets, by noon on Saturdays, May through August. Tours also by appointment (537 Jones St., San Francisco 94102; 564–7021).

SOUTH OF MARKET STREET

Locally known as "SoMa," this is the city's newest boom area. New restaurants, galleries, dance clubs, and avant-garde theaters open almost monthly. Overall, SoMa covers a large area, much of it very much in transition from its leather bar/hardware store/industrial warehouse past. To sample the best of the scene, try **Oasis,** 11th St. and Folsom (621–0264), a rock nightclub that serves good lunches and dinners; **Hamburger Mary's Organic Grill,** 1582 Folsom (626–5767), a good intro to the SoMa scene; **Taxi,** 374 11th St. (558–8294), a plain café with luscious food lauded in *Food & Wine* magazine; **Eddie Jacks,** 1151 Folsom, (626–2388), another *F&W* selection noted for its Italian/California menu; and **Clvb DV8,** 55 Natoma (777–1419), a disco with live entertainment Wednesday through Saturday nights. Check each of the above in advance on type of music, hours of operation, credit-card policy, cover charges, etc.

San Francisco is famous for its colorful sidewalk flower stands, and it's fun to visit the source—the Wholesale Flower Market at Sixth and Brannan streets. Most of the dealers welcome retail sales only on Saturday (9 to 11 A.M. is prime).

A few blocks away at the China Basin Building docks, 185 Berry, waits the 64-foot sailing yacht **Ruby** to take you on a 90-minute sailing lunch on the bay. At $25 per person, including a box lunch, it has to be the most fun for the least amount of money in town. At 12:30 P.M. daily, a blast on the yacht's horn opens the Third Street bridge, the sail goes up, and the course is set under the Bay Bridge, around Alcatraz, and along the Northern Waterfront before coming about off the Hyde Street Pier for the return to China Basin.

On Friday and Saturday at 6 P.M., the *Ruby* sails to Sausalito on a cocktail cruise ($25; cash bar). The *Ruby*'s owner-skipper is Joshua Pryor, winner of the 1982 race to the Farallon Islands, and the yacht is Coast Guard-certified and licensed. Reservations are recommended (861–2165), and topsiders and slacks are recommended. Cold-weather gear is aboard if you need it. Use the #2 entrance to the China Basin Building.

Blue-plate specials and the best hash in town arrive via poodle-skirted waitresses at glitzy **Max's Diner,** 311 Third St. (546–MAXS). Bubble gum comes with your bill. No reservations. Breakfast, lunch, and dinner are served daily; call for hours. AE/MC/V.

NOB HILL

Exploring

In June 1984, the 109-year-old cable car system returned to service after a $58.2-million overhaul. All three of the city's remaining cable-car lines crest at this famous hill, and the foot of Powell Street (at Market) is the turnaround for two. The **No. 60 Powell & Hyde line** climbs Nob Hill, swings west to Hyde Street, and clatters over Russian Hill to Victorian Park near Fisherman's Wharf, with access to the National Maritime Museum, Aquatic Park, and Ghirardelli Square.

The **No. 59 Powell & Mason line** also goes up Powell to Nob Hill and then jogs over to Mason Street for the run down to Bay Street, three blocks above the Embarcadero. Fisherman's Wharf is midway between the last stops of both lines and is an easy walk. The Hyde Street route passes the top of the "crookedest" street in town, nine steep curves on Lombard between Hyde and Leavenworth streets. You can walk down if you wish; a left turn on Leavenworth and a five-block walk then finds you at the wharf.

Both lines pass the **Cable Car Barn and Museum,** 1201 Mason at Washington (474–1887). Open daily from 10 A.M. to 5 P.M., this free museum includes the prototype of the first cable car, interesting old photos, and other SF memorabilia. Diagrams and a 16-minute film explain the basics of the system, and you can watch the steel cables at work.

The third cable-car line, the **No. 61 California,** runs from in front of the Hyatt Regency Hotel at Embarcadero Center (California & Market streets) to Van Ness Avenue, intersecting both Powell Street lines atop Nob Hill. A quick transfer, and you can be off to either the Northern Waterfront or Union Square.

Some random notes on cable-car riding: many of the gripmen are true SF characters who ring distinctively individual tattoos on the cable car bells. Folks who live alongside the car lines can tell who is going by, just by the sound. Also, don't jump on the cars when they are moving, hang on the outside, or stand directly behind the gripman. When he pulls back on the brake, you'll be clobbered, and that's not fun at all.

Bounded by California, Jones, Taylor, and Sacramento streets, Nob Hill became, in the 1870s, the lofty lair of the big four: C.P. Huntington, Charles Crocker, Mark Hopkins, and Leland Stanford. Railroad nabobs all, they built their mansions on this highest hill in town, financial kingpins of all they surveyed. Only one of those fabulous homes, the **James Flood brownstone** at the crest of California Street, survived the 1906 devastation. It remains a study in sturdy ostentation and is home to the very exclusive Pacific Union Club, locally referred to as the "P-U."

Another tie with the past is the deluxe **Mark Hopkins-Intercontinental Hotel,** built on the site of the Mark Hopkins mansion at No. 1 Nob Hill. In the late '30s the hotel's penthouse was converted into the famous **Top of the Mark** and immediately became *the* place in town to begin or end a love affair or an evening. Today, the Top of the Mark still holds its own against newcomers, a glass-walled study in bronze, brass, and tiny lights that meld into the night. Skip the buffet lunch and weekend brunch. Just go for drinks or a nightcap at the best address in town (392–3434).

Hotels

Across Mason from the PU sits the grande dame of San Francisco hotels, the **Fairmont.** While staying here is fine, it's fun just to enjoy the lobby, a baroque, gold-and-crimson wonder. You'll recognize it as the setting for the television series "Hotel." You can practice grand entrances on the gilded staircase, have yourself paged, or just enjoy a drink in the cosseting lobby bar. Ready to open in 1906 and then seriously damaged by the earthquake, the Fairmont greeted its first guest in 1907 and added a 29-story contemporary tower in 1961. Riding the exterior elevator to the Crown Room atop that tower is a "must" for tourists, day or night. Once there, however, settle for a drink; the food often doesn't match the view. For fine dining, you are better off in the handsome Squire Room off the main lobby (see the restaurant chapter), a *très* dressy affair.

Aside from the $5,000 penthouse suite (three bedrooms and baths, living and dining rooms, library, terrace, kitchen, etc.), rooms in the main building are $140–$180 single, $170–$210 double; tower rooms are $205–$230 single, $235–$260 double. (950 Mason St., San Francisco 94106; 415–772–5000 or 800–527–4727.)

The Stanford Court shares the 900 block of California St. with the Mark Hopkins and is considered by many one of the most notable hotels in the nation. Buried under honors and awards every year, this elegant 402-room hostelry is within the historic façade of the Stanford Court Apartments. They, in turn, were built in 1912 on the site of the Leland Stanford mansion, circa 1876. The massive retaining wall on the Powell Street side of the hotel is all that remains of that original home.

Expect to arrive in a large, circular courtyard-cum-fountain, topped with a handsome stained-glass dome. Expect a marble and ultra-upholstered lobby accented with antiques and fine works of art. Expect the ultimate in housekeeping—the walls are inspected for scuffs nightly and touched up the next day. And best of all, expect to feel at home.

Therein lies the secret to the Stanford Court's charm. A continued favorite of corporate executives, travel professionals, and celebrities who hate to leave, it's a hotel that doesn't seem like a hotel. If you can swing the $155–$215 single, $185–$240 double rate and can snag a reservation, do it. Expect a dressy atmosphere, however; jeans and sweatshirts may not raise an eyebrow with the staff, but those so dressed may feel uncomfortably out of place. (905 California St., San Francisco 94108; 415–989–3500; in CA: 800–622–0957; elsewhere: 800–227–4736.)

Dining

Fournou's Ovens—as unusual as the Stanford Court Hotel, which houses this fine restaurant—continues to specialize in roasts of veal, lamb, and beef cooked over oak in massive wall ovens, but the rest of the menu is moving toward a unique mix of cuisines, everything from a little French to the best of California. Copper plates set the tables, blue French provincial tiles face the ovens, and ropes of garlic, peppers, and bay hang here and there amid original art and antiques. The dining rooms are small, tucked-away terraces floored in red tile and fronted with curved iron grills; the wine cellar (21,000 bottles strong) offers one of the country's largest selections of California wines. In contrast, the bar is a contemporary conservatory, rich with ferns and rattan. Dinner is served nightly. 905 California (989–1910). AE/DC/MC/V.

Tiny **Nob Hill Café,** 1152 Taylor (776–6915), seems too humble to be on Nob Hill. The compact domain of Gerardo Boccara, it has seven tables inside and two tables outside—if weather permits. Gerardo reigns at his grill in the front window, turning out French bourgeois masterpieces like fresh scallops Niçoise. A blackboard menu lists the best of the day's fresh catch. Dinners range from $17.50 to $22.50 and include soup, salad, and vegetable. No bar, just the chef's selection of outstanding California and French wines. Open Tuesday through Saturday for lunch and dinner; reservations advised. MC/V.

FINANCIAL DISTRICT

Exploring

Centered on the intersection of California and Montgomery streets, the Financial District is for several blocks the somewhat staid realm of international banks, corporations, insurance companies, and the Pacific Coast Stock Exchange.

Prior to the gold strike of 1848, Montgomery Street was a muddy lane at the edge of the bay, and everything from what is now California Street to Columbus Avenue was water and long wharves. Then came the Gold Rush. Almost overnight, San Francisco became the threshold to fortune, and the sailing ships that brought the supplies and prospectors were abandoned at anchor, as crews headed for the gold fields. Converted into temporary stores and hotels, many of the slips became landlocked, as debris collected around them. Today, the bones of those ships underlie much of this Battery area, and Montgomery Street has enough $$-clout to be known as the Wall Street of the West.

Within these canyons of commerce are a handful of interesting restaurants and things to do. Two buildings stand out in particular. San Franciscans still have a love-hate relationship with the distinctive Transamerica Pyramid, 600 Montgomery. Don't bother with the limited view from the 27th-floor observation deck, but do enjoy the half-acre park at its eastern base, the only urban stand of redwoods in the world. Drop in at the **Bank Exchange** on the pyramid's ground floor for a weekday lunch; at 9 P.M., this becomes the **Park Exchange,** a good place to disco Wednesday through Saturday nights. The 779-foot-high Bank of America Building at Kearny and California streets is not only headquarters for the world's largest bank, it houses the **Carnelian Room** on the 52nd floor. (see *Dining* below).

Dining

Tadich Grill, The Original Cold Day Restaurant, 240 California St. (391–2373), is a Financial District institution, tracing its Yugoslavian roots to a tented coffee stand set up on a wharf in 1849. Don't ask the waiter for an explanation of the "Cold Day" label; just read the menu for this tidbit of San Francisco lore. Officially honored by the California Historical Society in 1981, Tadich's is popular among stockbrokers, business executives, and secretaries five days a week. No reservations are accepted, and the lunch line begins forming early and soon stretches around the corner. Things move swiftly, however, when the doors open at 11 A.M.

Inside, Tadich's is a no-nonsense place that puts first things first. The bar is smack in front, with tables and booths around and behind it on the left, and a counter stretching the length of the room on the right. Those folks waiting at the door usually want tables, so if counter service will do, move ahead and check out the situation.

The menu offers salads ($4–$13), charbroiled meats ($7.85–$13.75), and an enormous selection of fish dishes, ($6.95–$14.75). You are well off with any of the house specials, from homemade ravioli or corned beef hash to seafood cioppino in casserole, baked avocado and shrimp diablo, or a simple grilled double lamb chop. Tadich's is open weekdays only, 11 A.M. to 9 P.M., and no credit cards or checks are accepted.

The London Wine Bar, 415 Sansome St. (788–4811), was America's first when it opened in 1974, and it still sets the pace. Its wine list of 600 California and French labels is consistently rated among the top 100 in the country by trade magazines. Approximately two dozen wines from that cellar are featured daily at $2–$7 per five-ounce glass. Single bottles are sold to go at a reduction of $4 from the wine-list price, and there are discounts on case lots.

But this is far more than than a wine store. Financial District regulars, from messengers to managers, know it as a dark and cozy English pub where they can get an inexpensive sandwich, salad, or quiche lunch from 11:30 A.M. to 2:30 P.M. weekdays, or feast on fresh seafood from the icy seafood bar anytime during store hours: 11:30 A.M. to 9 P.M., Monday through Friday. Reservations are suggested during the peak of the lunch period. Closed Saturday and Sunday. AE/CB/DC/MC/V.

Hotels

Care for a bath with a view? The Mandarin rooms ($280 single or double) at **The Mandarin** hotel have tub-to-ceiling picture windows (with mini-blinds for the shy) in the bathrooms, and those facing north have a bridge-to-bridge panorama from the third-tallest building in the city. Bring your own binoculars or telescope to enjoy the other city-circling views from this luxurious aerie, on the top 11 floors of 345 California Center in the heart of the financial district. One of the city's finest restaurants, **Silks,** is on the mezzanine level. Standard rooms start at $185 single, $205 double, and suites are $750 and $900. (222 Sansome St., San Francisco 94104; 415–885–0999 or 800–622–0404.)

EMBARCADERO CENTER

The pace of the Financial District picks up at its eastern
limits at the **Embarcadero Center.** This $300-million city-
within-a-city bustles with more than 175 shops, restaurants,
galleries, and people-places, redefining both the life and business styles of San Francisco.

The keystone of the 51-acre Golden Gateway Redevelopment Area, Embarcadero Center has sparked other fresh construction within the Financial District as well as the refur-
bishment of the historic Ferry Building and its surrounding
promenades. Four of EC's skyscrapers are interconnected by
a series of handsome plazas and pedestrian malls, all highlighted by outstanding sculptures and other major art. Just
strolling and window-shopping here is a pleasure. Generally
speaking, EC's Three and Four offer more interesting shopping and restaurants than their earlier counterparts.

Dining

You can sample inventive California cuisine at **The Four
Star** on the podium level of Three EC (397–4422). The dignified peach-and-green rooms attract a dressy crowd, and the
food ranges from unusual appetizers to fish, salads, pasta, and
daily specials. Open for lunch and dinner, Monday through
Friday. Prime-time reservations are a necessity. AE/
DC/MC/V.

You can eat outside at **The Holding Co.** on the podium
level of Two EC (986–0797). This bar-that-serves-food has
a clubby feel (no minors allowed) and offers lunch and dinner,
Monday through Friday. This is a TGIF place for Financial
District drones and developers alike, particularly the under-
40 crowd. AE/MC/V.

The New Eagle Bar and Cafe on the podium level of EC Four
(397–2056) not only serves breakfast; it may be the only EC
eatery open seven days a week. Hamburgers are the big draw
here, along with a good salad bar, large steak sandwiches, and
some other light entrées. The staff is young, lively, and friendly, and the hours are 7 A.M. to 4 P.M. AE/MC/V.

Scott's Carriage House, also on the podium level of Three EC (433–7444), serves outstanding seafood, salads, and poultry in a traditional English club atmosphere—try for the outdoor patio tables on a fine day. Scott's is popular with the Financial District carriage trade. Reservations are a must for lunch Monday through Friday, dinner Tuesday through Saturday. AE/DC/MC/V.

One of the most elegant Cantonese restaurants in town is **Harbor Village,** lobby level of EC Four (781–8833). The only U.S. branch of the Harbor Village in Hong Kong, it offers dim sum at lunch and such goodies as ginger crab in black-bean sauce at dinner daily. AE/DC/MC/V.

Aside from shopping, restaurants, etc., the best part of Embarcadero Center is the vast Justin Herman Plaza, on the bay side of EC Four and adjacent to the Hyatt Regency. Lined with sidewalk cafés, this is where everyone from tycoon to typist catches some rays at lunch and socializes after work. When the weather is nice, the street people are out in force—artists, musicians, mimes, vendors—both on the open-air stage of the Plaza Theatre and among the crowds, and a walk through the Vaillancourt Fountain will be a relaxing break from a harrowing morning of shopping.

Hotels

The fifth part of Embarcadero Center is the 803-room **Hyatt Regency,** which, because of its great style and location, is one of the most enjoyable places to stay in San Francisco. The standard guest rooms are $218 single, $248 double, and you should request a balcony room for a great view. The 16th-floor Regency Club ($238–$268) comes with concierge, Continental breakfast, and assorted frills. (No. 5 Embarcadero Center, San Francisco 94111; 415–788–1234 or 800–228–9000.)

Even if you don't stay here, come for the fun. Just walking through the soaring atrium lobby with its fountains, sculpture, and babbling brook is an experience, and the free Friday afternoon tea dances (5:30 to 8:30) are grand fun.

Both the California Street cable car terminus and the Embarcadero Center station of the BART/Metro subway are directly outside the Hyatt on Market Square. Muni surface buses also connect EC with the Downtown/Union Square Area, Civic Center, and other parts of town.

On The Bay

Enjoying San Francisco's bay from the financial district and Embarcadero Center is easy—the ferries are back, and the city's most enduring landmark, The Ferry Building (circa 1895) near the foot of Market, has a new lease on life, thanks to the Golden Gateway Redevelopment. Ferries run daily to Sausalito ($3.50 one-way) and Larkspur ($2.20–$3) in Marin County. Call 332–6600 for departure times. Other bay boat services to Sausalito, Alcatraz, Angel Island, Vallejo, and Tiburon depart from the Fisherman's Wharf area. Call 546–2815 for schedules. See the Fisherman's Wharf chapter for details.

THE GOLDEN GATEWAY, JACKSON SQUARE, AND THE BAY

North of Embarcadero Center lie the Golden Gateway and Jackson Square. The latter is a fashionable business address bounded by Columbus, Pacific, Battery, and Washington streets.

Originally a small slough, this area was filled with ship ballast and hulks during the Gold Rush days and became the commercial heart of town. Gold and Balance streets were named for their use—miners dumped their gold pokes and nuggets there for assaying and weighing—and the U.S. Customs House was at 630 Sansome. The stout brick buildings were built to last, and they did—right through the 1906 quake. Today, they have been refurbished into sophisticated and handsome offices, wholesale decorator showrooms, restaurants, and a handful of retail shops.

Jackson Square is an official historic district, and 17 of the old buildings are designated landmarks. Wander into Hotaling Place, a charming alley in the 400 block of Jackson. This leads to the rear of 722–728 Montgomery, a lavishly rococo Victorian compound that houses the legal offices of "King of Torts" Melvin Belli and associates. Don't be alarmed if a cannon goes off and a Jolly Roger is flying in the breeze. That means lawyer Belli has just won another case!

The best of the city's antique dealers have opened shops in the Jackson Square area recently, primarily on Jackson and Sansome streets. Browsers are warmly welcomed, and the ambience of the entire area has greatly improved.

Dining

Jackson Square and nearby Levi Plaza are fertile fields for fine dining. The restaurants are brimming with upwardly mobile types from the Financial District for weekday lunch and dinner, so if you want the good food minus crowds, try dinner on Saturday or Sunday. On the other hand, if you love the action, Friday after 5 P.M. is the peak of the week.

Adjacent to both Embarcadero Center and Jackson Square is a green park known as **Golden Gateway Commons,** and beyond that lies one of SF's rage restaurants, **Square One,** 190 Pacific, at Front Street (788–1110). Owner Joyce Goldstein is chief creator and taster of a daily menu that features Mediterranean classics with unusual seasonings, all based on the best of the fresh foods found in that day's market. The atmosphere is subdued—it doesn't try to upstage the food—and all manner of folk come here in search of a fine dining experience. There's a nonsmoking section, plus a selection of wines by the glass. Open Monday through Friday for lunch, for dinner nightly. Reservations are essential. AE/MC/V.

Another Goldstein venture, **Caffe Quadro,** is next door at 180 Pacific (398–1777). Italian casual in both atmosphere and food, this is a good spot for pizza, sandwiches, or a calzone lunch on weekdays. The menu changes daily. MC/V.

Diners continue to flourish in San Francisco, and the flossiest is **Fog City Diner,** at 1300 Battery at Lombard (982–2000), across from Levi Plaza. This gleaming Art Deco takeoff on an American classic applies similar twists to the menu, featuring new-era American cuisine and a great oyster bar. You may want to order all the appetizers out of sheer curiosity. Reservations necessary; lunch and dinner daily. MC/V.

If the lines are long at the above spots, try either the newly refurbished **MacArthur Park,** 607 Front St. (398–5700), for tasty Americana (fresh fish, smoked game, steak, and ribs), or a high-tech trattoria called **Ciao,** around the corner at 230 Jackson (982–9500) and half a world away in cuisine (Northern Italian pastas and entrées). Both eateries take AE/MC/V.

CIVIC CENTER

Exploring

San Francisco's vast **Civic Center** is one of the handsomest in America, and, thanks to some fresh investment, it's becoming fun to explore.

San Franciscans love their beautiful domed **City Hall,** even when they have to come in to pay their taxes. Admire the interior on your own, or take the free tour given at noon on Thursday (558–3770). The brick mall between City Hall and Market Street becomes a farmer's market every Wednesday and Sunday from 8:00 A.M. to 3:00 P.M.

The **War Memorial Opera House** is just what an opera house should be—grand in the classic sense of the word. Why not hire a limo and use the carriage entrance with the rest of the toffs?

During the day, the Opera House is reflected in the circular glass façade of the new, $28.5 million **Louise M. Davies Symphony Hall,** but at night this new theater twinkles with a personality all its own. Contemporary and welcoming, where the Opera House is regal, it's been a hit since its opening in late 1980.

Guided tours of the entire Performing Arts Center—Davies Hall, the Opera House, and Herbst Theatre in the adjacent Veterans Memorial Building—are given for $3 at 30-minute intervals from 10 A.M. to 2:30 P.M. on Mondays (552–8338). There are also tours of Davies Hall on Wednesday and Saturday only.

Modern art lovers should not miss the **Museum of Modern Art** on two upper floors of the War Memorial Veterans Building. The collection includes works by Calder, Motherwell, Matisse, Klee, and other major figures, and local and regional artists often are featured in the special shows. Admission is $3.50 (Thursday evenings are free), and the museum is closed on Monday. Ask about guided tours (863–8800).

The completion of the new concert hall jazzed up the neighborhood. The 300 block of Hayes begins with the Hayes Street Grill and ends with Ivy's Restaurant and Bar (restaurant chapter). In between are antique shops, an art gallery, and two fun places for snacks. Two blocks north on Van Ness from Civic Center is the new Opera Center development.

Dining

The food is fine any time, but the fun begins after 6:30 P.M. and continues all evening at **Max's Opera Café,** 601 Van Ness in Opera Center. The waiters and waitresses are professional singers who are just looking for that big chance and paying the bills by singing and serving at Max's in the meantime. More than 600 auditioned for the 40 original openings, so you may hear a future star during one of the informal shows.

Basically an upscale deli with high-tech overtones, Max's has an extensive, inventive menu of salads, sandwiches, and hot dishes, with daily blackboard specials. The atmosphere is upholstered casual, one of those places you would take either your lover or an aging aunt. Open daily, serving everything from brunch to after-theater supper. Reservations advised (771–7300). AE/CB/MC/V.

If your palate can pick the extra virgin olive oil from the *ordinaire,* then you shouldn't miss the **Zuni Cafe and Grill,** 1658 Market (552–2522). Rather Spartan in its southwestern decor, this trendy place features southern French and northern Italian dishes and utilizes a brick oven fired with white oak for grilling poultry and fish. The best tables for viewing both the cooks in the open kitchen and the other customers are along the balcony upstairs, and they are worth asking for when you reserve. The seafood bar has its own menu, and the wine list is extensive and well-priced by the bottle or the glass. The art (which is for sale) tends toward the bizarre, and the clientele sometimes follows suit. Expect everything from evening dress to jeans. Open for Sunday brunch, lunch Tuesday through Saturday, and dinner Tuesday through Sunday. AE/MC/V.

Jeremiah Tower, one of the leading lights of cuisine Americana, puts forth fresh lunch and dinner menus daily at **Stars,** 150 Redwood (parallels the 500 block of Golden Gate Ave. at Van Ness; 861–7827). The open kitchen is fascinating, and the food has great imagination. A pianist adds a touch of romance during the dinner hours, and visiting celebrities are often scattered around the dining room. Lunch is served weekdays, dinner nightly, and there's also an excellent oyster bar. Best bets: go with your waiter's recommendations and the house drinks listed on the mirror behind the bar. AE/DC/MC/V. In a hurry? Tower now operates **Starfish,** an inexpensive fish and chips take-out next door.

Chinatown and North Beach

Exploring

At first this may seem the odd couple of San Francisco sight-seeing—pagodas to pizzerias, ginseng to gelato. What the Chinese and Italian communities have in common is Grant Avenue and many of its side streets, and the boundary lines tend to blend and overlap. It's possible and fun to wander between the two. This may be the only place in the country where you can eat French food served by a Chinese waiter in an Italian restaurant.

Officially, Chinatown is bounded by Stockton, Kearny, Bush, and Broadway—16 square blocks in which the street signs are subtitled in Chinese characters.

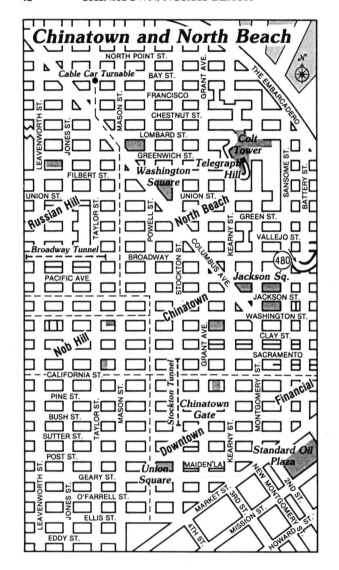

Chinatown and North Beach

This is the largest Chinese community outside the Orient, the Hong Kong of the Western Hemisphere. The definitive entrance is the dragon gate at Grant and Bush streets, one block over (Post) and two blocks up (Grant) from Union Square. Grant Street narrows here, and the next three blocks are lined with shops selling everything from Indian jewelry to fine imports from mainland China.

Don't walk Grant Street and think you've seen all of Chinatown. Catch side streets or the early morning market scene along Stockton Street.

The best way to see Chinatown is with a native. There are commercial evening tours (skip the dinner option) that do a good job, but the best and least expensive ($9) are the **Chinese Heritage Walks.** These are guided by the Chinese Culture Foundation staff at 2 P.M. on Saturdays and leave from their headquarters on the third floor of the Holiday Inn, 750 Kearny (986–1822). Advance reservations are required. Stops include the Chinese Historical Society of America, t'ai chi ch'uan studio, Chinese temple, fortune-cookie factory, herb store, and other points of architectural interest. The museum of the **Chinese Historical Society of America,** 17 Adler Pl., focuses on the role of the Chinese in the growth of San Francisco and the West. Closed on Sunday and Monday (391–1188). Open Tuesday through Saturday, 1–5 P.M.

Dining

There is no better introduction to good and simple Chinese food than a dim sum (pleasure of the heart) lunch. But one look at the mystery bundles on a dim sum selection tray, and you may wish you had settled for a peanut-butter sandwich. Confucius says take the **Chinatown Culinary Walk/ Luncheon** led by the Chinese Culture Foundation. Stops include markets, stores, factories, and a dim sum restaurant where all will be explained, including the mystery of eating with chopsticks. The tours are $18 by reservation only (986–1822).

If you've already had a cultural tour of Chinatown, brave the dim sum scene on your own. You can eat very well for less than $8, even if the only thing you recognize is the egg roll. The larger restaurants, like **Grand Palace,** 950 Grant Ave. (982–3705), cater to tourists and businessmen and will offer patient explanations and forks when needed. Smaller restaurants, such as **Yank Sing,** 427 Battery (362–1640), have a neighborhood clientele and can be impatient as you question what's what. In all dim sum restaurants, the play's the same. Large trays or trolleys of food are constantly circulated around the room. You point to the one you want, and your bill is calculated by the number and type of plates you accumulate. Happily, each offering is small and inexpensive ($1–$2.50), so if you don't care for it, you haven't invested much. On Saturday, dim sum is a tradition for Chinese families; you'll see three and four generations, all chattering away in Cantonese while the chopsticks fly.

Sam Wo, 813 Washington St. (982–0596), is another Chinatown institution, an upstairs soup kitchen well known for a feisty waiter, the late Edsel Ford Wong. The menu must be his handiwork: "All food. No booze, No BS, No jive, No coffee, milk, soft drinks or fortune cookies." It also tells you to "Be precise and concise on every little thing." So take the hint and promptly order the house speciality, *jook.* This is a thick rice soup ($2.25) to which you add pork, chicken, fish, or beef ($1.05–$2.90). Sam Wo also introduced Chinese crullers to San Francisco; order them with the *jook.* Other specialties include fried won ton soup and marinated raw-fish salad. If you are marveling at the low prices, you haven't seen Sam Wo's. It isn't new, decorated, or soliciting business. You enter through a narrow kitchen on the street level and climb a flight of decrepit stairs to tiny eating areas on the second and third floor. The whole place looks like a storage shed left over from the Tong wars. Ignore your common sense and GO (unless it's Sunday, when it's closed). Eating at Sam Wo's is famous, fun, and very San Francisco. No credit cards are honored, needless to say.

One block and light years away from Sam Wo's is **Imperial Palace,** 919 Grant Ave. (982–4440). When the advance billing reads "the most exclusive Chinese restaurant in the country," you know it's time to get out the charge cards. From the petite hostesses in their sexy satin cheongsams to the waiters in their tuxes, this is a *very nice place.* It's also a very dark place, so you may want to palm a flashlight to read the menu. The food is superb—prawns in lobster sauce, shredded scallop soup, lichee chicken, and other treats—and the service is even better. You won't have to use chopsticks unless you want to. Complete dinners range from the Imperial Treat at $18.95 to the Emperor's Gourmet at $37.95, but there's plenty to select from à la carte. Open daily for lunch and dinner; reservations advised. AE/CB/DC/MC/V.

NORTH BEACH

Exploring

Cathay gives way to Italy as Grant Avenue crosses Pacific going north and enters North Beach. The intersection of Grant and Broadway with Columbus is not only T&A corner, it's also the beginning of what writer Herbert Gold calls "the longest-running Bohemian operetta in America."

The cradle of the Beat generation of the late 1950s, North Beach remains the home ground of poets, painters, free spirits, and thousands of Italians. By day, this is Little Italy—bakeries and gelato stores, housewives shopping for pasta and the makings of scallopine and antipasti, babies and old men basking in the sun of Washington Square. By night, it's the city alive, a colorful mix of bistros, cabarets, coffeehouses, and restaurants.

Columbus Avenue remains the neighborhood's baseline as it angles from the Financial District to the Fisherman's Wharf area, separating Chinatown and Russian Hill on the southwest from North Beach. With the exception of several good restaurants, Broadway is sleazy sex-club row, featuring the same headliners for decades. The best of North Beach strolling is found along Columbus from Broadway to and around Washington Square, on Union and Green streets, and on upper Grant Avenue as it climbs to Lombard Street and Telegraph Hill. Across Columbus lies Jackson Square.

Old San Francisco lives on at the **San Francisco Brewing Co.** at Columbus and Pacific, with its unusual vertical fans and flamed mahogany back bar, made for the Andromeda Saloon, which opened on this Barbary Coast site in 1907 (155 Columbus, 434–3344). Jack Dempsey was the bouncer here in 1913–14, and "Baby Face" Nelson was arrested in the bar's stockroom in 1929. The big copper vats that now decorate the dining area brew SF's only locally produced lager and pilsner beer. Lunch and dinner daily. AE/MC/V.

The next block holds the famous hangout of the Beat generation, Lawrence Ferlinghetti's **City Lights Bookstore,** 261 Columbus (362–8193). Stop in and browse in this almost-historic landmark—it's open until midnight. Next door is Vesuvio cafe, another survivor. Across the street at 242 Columbus is **Tosca's,** a dark and ancient bar where you can buy an espresso, Irish coffee, or cappuccino after 7 P.M. and listen to vintage opera on the Wurlitzer.

Molinari's, 373 Columbus, is the ultimate in Italian delis, and on Saturday it's a take-a-number operation. Go instead on a midweek day when you can marvel at the towers of olive oil tins, the banks of Italian wines, the rounds and mounds of cheese and freshly-made pastas, and then order some sandwiches.

You can climb up Telegraph Hill to Coit Tower, but it's much better to ride up and then walk down the Filbert Steps to Levi Plaza and the Embarcadero. An alternate path follows Montgomery, Union, and Kearny down another side of the hill and ends up on Broadway at Enrico's—good planning! If you haven't a car, the No. 39 Coit bus comes down Union Street, picks up in front of the Ristorante Fior d'Italia at Washington Square, and then goes up to Coit Tower before continuing on to Fisherman's Wharf.

But before you go, take time to explore the 1200–1400 blocks of upper Grant. Amid the gelato shops and bakeries, you'll find **The Saloon,** 1232 Grant, (989–7666), established in 1861 and recently saved from demolition. It looks like a stage set from the Clark Gable/Jeanette MacDonald movie, *San Francisco,* with Blackie just out of sight. Blues here nightly, plus jazz on Sunday. The next corner (Vallejo Street) is home to the **Cafe Trieste** (392–6739), a coffeehouse with operatic overtones run by the Giotta clan.

A touch of old San Francisco lives at the tiny **Italian-French Baking Co.,** 1501 Grant. Their sour and crusty sourdough bread was judged the best in the city in a blind judging at the 1987 San Francisco Fair.

Next up is an overdose of nostalgia at **Quantity Postcards,** 1441 Grant (986–8866), where at least half of the 10,000 different postcards in stock are pre-1961 collector's items. Across the street you can buy a foreign-legion hat, baseball cards, or other forgettable trivia at the **Shlock Shop.** The

Savoy Tivoli, 1434 Grant, is an indoor/outdoor coffee and dessert bar, complete with tin palm trees, potted petunias, pool tables, funky blues music, and shows upstairs. New antique shops and fashion boutiques are sprouting up here, slowly changing the face of this special neighborhood.

Dining

Like a diamond in the dime store, **Café Jacqueline** stands out at 1454 Grant (981–5565). Small, simple, and spotless, this is the perfect showcase for towering soufflés, the house specialty. A native of the Bordeaux region of France, Jacqueline turns out soufflés with the effort ordinary cooks expend on boiling water. The daily specials and fresh fruit soufflés in season (raspberry, peach, etc.) can run as high as $22, but the menu also offers mushroom and spinach, or prosciutto and mushroom, soufflés at $15. Each is big enough for two persons. The rest rooms are out back, worth mentioning only because a trip there lets you pass through the tiny kitchen and watch the chef at work. Open for à la carte dinner Wednesday through Saturday; brunch on weekends. Reservations are suggested. Closed July and August. AE/CB/DC/MC/V.

Rain or shine, there's almost always a line outside **Little Joe's,** 523 Broadway (982–7639). Your best bet is to go before or after the prime lunch and dinner hours. Eschew the tables in the dining room in favor of a counter seat where you can watch the cooks creating the house specials, among them fish stew, chicken polenta, and a wonderful sautéed vegi-creation. Herbs and wine fly, and you'll end up with a lesson in Italian cooking. Meals range from $6–$11, and no credit cards are accepted.

For something lighter or just a prime view of the passing scene, cross the street to **Enrico's,** 504 Broadway (392–6220). This is as close as San Francisco comes to the sidewalk cafés of Paris, and Enrico, a beret-wearing, bear-size man, usually is on-scene. Sodas, malts, wine, and beer are sold, and the house specialties include homemade ravioli—James Beard praised one exotic version called Angel Wings—and Enrico's Original Ambrosia, a mix of coffee, Galliano, and cognac. Go most anytime. Enrico's is open from 11:30 A.M. to 3 A.M., and there's live jazz Thursday through Saturday nights. AE/MC/V.

James Beard also put his stamp of approval on **Vanessi's,** 498 Broadway (421–0890/0891). Though this San Francisco institution sounds and is Italian, it handles California food equally well. The Provimi veal and fresh fish are daily specials, and a seat at the counter will allow you to watch the toque-topped cooks doing their thing at the grill. The glass-fronted wine cellar, 2,000 bottles strong, makes an interesting bar back; the dining room atmosphere is dark and soothing, very popular with businessmen at both lunch and dinner. You'll need reservations, even for a counter seat. Open weekdays for lunch and dinner, Saturday for dinner. This is a good place for an after-theater snack. AE/CB/DC/MC/V.

You won't find spaghetti or garlic bread at **RAF,** 478 Green, but you will find the city's most swank Italian dining scene. Part contemporary, part Tuscan ruin, this open-raftered place is known for its bread salad, variety of antipasti, country dishes like osso buco, and large-sized spumoni desserts. There's a full bar, plus Italian, and Californian wines. Open for lunch on weekdays, dinner nightly. (362–1999). AE/CB/DC/MC/V.

For an eyeful of Italian handicrafts and kitchen things, linger at **Biordi Art Imports,** 412 Columbus (392–8096). If you fall in love with a Majolica plate or weaken and buy a Neopolitan cappuccino machine, they'll happily ship it home for you. Next up are the **Caffe Roma** and **Calzone's,** both semi-sidewalk eateries, thanks to large sliding windows that bring in the outdoors. Across the street is **The Puccini,** 411 Columbus, a sleek and friendly coffeehouse that is winning over the North Beach regulars.

Detour onto the 500 block of Green Street long enough to find and marvel at the **Caffe Sport** (see the restaurant chapter) and to buy breadsticks or loaves of bread shaped like hands at the **Danila Bakery.** Across Columbus on Green is **Club Fugazi,** a former Italian social hall now headlining the zany "Beach Blanket Babylon" (see Nightlife below).

Powell intersects Columbus at Washington Square, the piazza of North Beach. This shady block of grass, benches, and monuments fronts handsome Saints Peter and Paul Cathedral, the neighborhood's religious heart, and is a good place to picnic with sandwiches from Molinari's. You can almost drink the scent of coffee in the air, and for dessert there's *cioc-*

colato, zabaglione, or amaretto gelati (Italian ices) across the street at the gelateria on the corner of Filbert and Columbus.

Singer & Foy Wines has established a cultural beachhead in North Beach at 1821 Powell (989–0396) just off Washington Square. Although they open selected bottles and print an advance schedule, you can taste anything in the stock by arrangement. Tastes are 10 percent of the bottle price, and a 5-oz. glass usually is in the $1.50–$2.50 price range. A number of the French wines are exclusive to this shop in San Francisco, and there are some select Italian, Oregon, and California labels as well. Closed Sunday. MC/V.

There's usually life and laughter at the **Washington Square Bar and Grill**, 1707 Powell St. (982–8123). Long a favorite with the city's literati and journalistic types—Walter Cronkite may be in the next booth—this saloon is noisy but good. Both lunch and dinner menus are a mix of Northern Italian and Continental food. The bar is large and basic, food is served until 11 P.M. (Sunday brunch from 10 A.M. to 3 P.M., too), and the atmosphere is strictly good time. Wear what you want. AE/MC/V.

Ristorante Fior d'Italia anchors one side of Washington Square at 601 Union St. (986–1886). This is San Francisco's oldest Italian restaurant, established in 1886 and never closed. When the original Broadway site was destroyed in the earthquake, they just set up a tent in the rubble and began to stir the pots. You'll want to dress up some here to match the ambience of this dignified cream-and-wine dining room with dark leather banquettes, indirect lighting, fresh flowers, and enough staff to serve the president. The menu offers Northern Italian specialties, with emphasis on calamari and other California seafood. Jackets for the gentlemen, please, but ties are optional. Open weekdays for lunch, nightly for dinner. AE/CB/DC/MC/V.

Ever eaten in a ravioli factory? **The Cafferata Ravioli Factory**, 700 Columbus (392–7544), has 100 years of pasta experience and sells 27 varieties either to go or eat there. Lunch on-site is recommended, preferably in one of the two cubbyholes that flank the main door. The menu also offers calamari salad, sausages, cappuccino, espresso, cold beers, and wines.

If you want to see ravioli being made, early mornings are best. Open for lunch and dinner daily. MC/V.

Hotels

The Washington Square Inn, also facing the park, was designed and decorated by the same stylish hand as the Inn on Union Square. Popular with young professionals in town for the weekend, this bed-and-breakfast inn has a country French air, courtesy of the English and French antiques in each of the guest rooms. Numbers 7 and 8 overlook the square, and Continental breakfast can be served in your room, or you can join the other guests in the lobby commons room and get acquainted. Tea is served from 4 to 7 P.M., and there is a concierge to help with anything from theater tickets to picnic arrangements. Some of the 15 rooms have twin beds, others have doubles, kings, or queens, so ask what's available when you reserve. Five of the smaller rooms upstairs share hall baths. Rates range from $55 to $150 single, $65 to $160 double, and reservations are suggested as far in advance as possible. (1660 Stockton St., San Francisco 94133; 415–981–4220.)

Although a little more commercial with the bed-and-breakfast idea, the **Millefiori Inn** is another good choice in North Beach lodgings. The 15 rooms ($65–$75 single, $75–$85 double) have only showers, and not all sport a closet! White shutters cover the bay windows overlooking Columbus, and each of the rooms has a different flower theme. Those at the back are the quietest. The brass is always shiny, the Florentine ceramic chandeliers are charming, and the Continental breakfast is served two doors down at the Caffe Roma, owned by the same management. It's easy to miss this neat-as-a-pin spot, so look for the old-fashioned, four-faced jeweler's clock in the 400 block of Columbus in front of the inn's entry. (444 Columbus Ave., San Francisco, CA 94133; 415–433–9111.)

Northern Waterfront

The Northern Waterfront stretches from the southern terminus of the Golden Gate Bridge to the Ferry Building and is best divided into at least three fun expeditions. Fisherman's Wharf, from Ghirardelli Square to Pier 39, is every tourist's first destination in San Francisco and the best place to start. Fort Mason combines well with a day on Marina Green, a picnic at the Palace of Fine Arts, and solving some of life's mysteries at the Exploratorium. Then comes an exhilarating day on the Golden Gate itself, with the Presidio and Fort Point thrown in to sweeten the pot.

Even more fun comes with a ferry ticket. Day trips to Angel Island, Alcatraz, Tiburon, and Sausalito are inexpensive and memorable ways to enjoy San Francisco and its bay.

Getting to the Northern Waterfront is easy. Columbus Avenue, the Embarcadero, and Powell, Taylor, and Leavenworth streets all end in the Fisherman's Wharf area, although the last three go over a few hills in the process. From Union

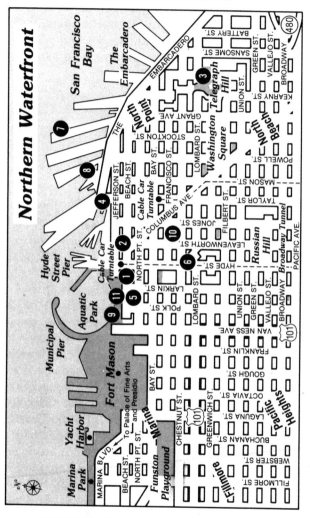

Points of Interest

1) Buena Vista Café
2) The Cannery
3) Coit Tower
4) Fisherman's Wharf
5) Ghirardelli Square
6) Lombard Street
7) Pier 39
8) *Balclutha*
9) Maritime Museum
10) San Francisco Art Institute
11) Victorian Park

Square, the No. 60 Powell and Hyde line cable car is a straight shot to Victorian Park and the National Maritime Museum, and the No. 59 Powell and Mason line cable car ends at Bay Street, three blocks from the wharf. A number of bus routes serve Fisherman's Wharf from various parts of town. Check with your hotel personnel or a Muni map for the best choice for you.

FISHERMAN'S WHARF

Exploring

You'll find the fishing boats massed along Jefferson Street between piers 45 and 47, but the term "Fisherman's Wharf" is generally used to cover everything from Pier 39 to Aquatic Park. For a look at the way the wharf was before tourist-time, walk down Fish Alley (on the bay side of Jefferson, between Jones and Leavenworth). You may see a trawler off-loading that day's catch on the backside of Pier 45 or fishermen mending their nets.

There no longer is party-boat fishing for either rock cod or albacore, but if you want to try your luck at fishing for salmon, you'll find numerous party boats lined up at the wharf along Jefferson Street by mid-afternoon. Walk along and see which one appeals to you; there may be room aboard the next day. The total cost varies little between the companies. **Captain Ron's Pacific Charters** (285–2000), for example, operates five large boats in all-day (seasonal) pursuit of this silver fish ($38). Bait and hooks are included (they even do the dirty work for you), and your fish are cleaned and bagged in heavy plastic. Rod-and-reel rental is $5 additional, plus you will need a one-day license ($4.50). This same firm offers salmon trolling from 3:30 P.M. until dusk in summer for $35, plus license and equipment. Your catch can be smoked or frozen for the flight home.

The sidewalk crab pots will be steaming along Jefferson and around the corner on Taylor, the crabs stacked like cords of wood. If there are rubber bands around the crabs, they probably have been frozen and shipped in. November through mid-April is California's Dungeness crab season, and the crabs then are fresh and sweet. A take-out crab cocktail is inexpensive fun anytime, but check the sauce—it can be a watery disappointment.

Even more fun is seeing the sights from the air. Commodore Helicopters flies every few minutes, 9 A.M. to sunset daily, from Pier 43 on your choice of three loops. The four-minute flight ($20) goes over the bay, around Alcatraz, and near Angel Island. The 10-minute loop ($40) goes around Alcatraz and over the Golden Gate Bridge. The 15-minute trip ($60) rounds Alcatraz en route to Sausalito, the Golden Gate, Cliff House, and Seal Rocks. There's almost always a line for the short $20 flight, and all trips have a two-person minimum. No credit cards are accepted. The flights are at their best in the late afternoon and just before sunset, but you run the risk of fog cancellation (981–4832).

Moving west on Jefferson from the wharf, you'll pass the Anchorage—stop in for shopping and some deep-fried sourdough puffs—and The Cannery en route to the National Maritime Museum, Aquatic Park, and Ghirardelli Square.

Built in 1894 by the Del Monte Company, the old brick walls of **The Cannery** now house 50 shops, galleries, and restaurants, thanks to an imaginative $8-million conversion in 1967. For inexpensive food of every description, shop the many stands inside, and, for snacks and entertainment, settle into the shady courtyard. The patio stage is a showcase for magicians, mimes, clowns, etc., at various times of day and is a good place to relax.

Nice to know: you can cover the waterfront in old-time style. Horse-drawn carriage tours leave Pier 41 daily starting at 1 P.M. and the destination is your choice. You can cover the five blocks of Fisherman's Wharf (8 min., $8 per couple) or trot down to the Hyatt Regency at Embarcadero Center and back to Ghirardelli Square (60 min., $50 per couple). For information, call 398–0857.

Don't miss the five historic ships docked at the **Hyde Street Pier,** part of the Golden Gate National Recreation Area. Each of the old ships represents a different phase of seafaring on the Pacific Coast, and, for some, like the ferry boat *Eureka* (last run in 1957) and the tug *Hercules* (last shove in 1962), the past was only yesterday. The *Balclutha,* a square-rigged Cape Horn sailing ship built in 1886, gives a feel for what San Francisco's waterfront looked like at the turn of the century. For her centennial she received a much-needed renovation, new rigging, and new main mast, and once again she is the queen of the docks.

Touring the pier and ships is $2 for adults, $1 for children. There are guided tours by the park staff and ongoing restoration work to watch. Best-of-show prizes go both to the houseboat that vignettes vacation life in Sausalito and the Delta two generations ago and to the *C.W. Thayer,* a wooden-hulled, three-master schooner built in 1895 and used to haul lumber from the dog-hole ports of the Mendocino coast. The pier itself is historic—in pre-bridge days it was the ferry-boat gateway to Berkeley and Sausalito. (556–6435).

The sidewalks between the Anchorage and Aquatic Park are street-artist row. You can have your caricature done in living color in one minute for $3, help feed a local clown by paying him 25 cents to pose with you for a picture, or play the "Band in the Box" by stuffing a dollar into a brightly painted packing crate. Serious artists of merit also show their wares in the park, along with some hawkers with unusual crafts. This is no fly-by-night, low-class fair. One man has been selling smoking pipes made of dried chicken legs—one $15 number gives the freeway salute—in the same spot for 14 years!

In the early morning, Aquatic Park is a quite different show, as the exercise and jogging headquarters for the neighborhood. Hardy souls can swim daily in the chilly waters off the small beach, and the curving municipal pier is a nice walk anytime. The **National Maritime Museum** at the top of the park is filled with models and exhibits that trace San Francisco's nautical history.

The **Carousel Museum** is another great stop (655 Beach at Hyde; 928–0550; open daily). Brimming with the oldest and most elaborate examples of carved merry-go-round animals in the country, it also has restoration workshops and a rare Wurlitzer Band Organ.

Hotels

The **Sheraton at Fisherman's Wharf** is a lively place to stay. Brimming with families and foreign travelers in the summer, conventions in September and October, and corporate travelers year-round, the lobby often seems one big party. The atmosphere is set by a contemporary blend of redwood, brick, and glass, with a few antiques and oriental rugs scattered around to warm things up, and there is a large pool in a recreation courtyard. The staff lives it up in costume to match special wharf-area events, and the in-house bar, Chanen's, often has theme nights and live music. The climate-controlled guest rooms are large and well-furnished with either kings or two doubles, and those on the fourth floor have canted ceiling windows with Roman shades, à la artists' lofts. Rates are $115–$180, depending on the size of room and party. (2500 Mason St., San Francisco 94133; 415–362–5500 or 800–325–3535.)

The **Holiday Inn** is another good choice at the wharf. Contemporary and airy, it offers some nice touches like free in-room HBO movies, massaging shower heads, heated outdoor pool and sun deck. The deluxe rooms with king-size beds are $134 single, $150 double; standard "no surprise" rooms are $123 single, $139 double. Check on packages. (1300 Columbus Ave., San Francisco 94133; 415–771–9000 or 800–465–4329.)

The classy, 256-room **San Francisco Marriott at Fisherman's Wharf** tones up the neighborhood considerably. Dignified on the exterior, it's a sumptuous mix of gleaming brass, glass, and marble played against terra-cotta tones throughout the lobby. Even if there's no room in the inn, don't miss drinks in the lobby piano bar after a day on the wharf. Rates are $135–$195 single, $151–$210 double, but drop to $115 on weekends. (1250 Columbus Ave., San Francisco 94122; 415–775–7555 or 800–228–9290.)

Dining

San Francisco's love affair with food has finally reached the wharf. Castagnola's sports a new menu that emphasizes light sauces and fresh ingredients, and Allioto's wine list is superb, thanks to the fact that its general manager is one of eight master sommeliers in America.

Scoma's also is considered one of the best. Tucked away at the end of Fish Alley on Pier 47, it is always busy. Come prepared to wait. All the fish is fresh, much of it from their own boat, and everything is prepared Italian style to order, sometimes a very lengthy process. The menu is the same for lunch and dinner, and the daily specials ($9.95–$12.95) never last after 2 P.M. Even with your name on the list, you can count on a 20- to 30-minute wait (771–4383). AE/CB/DC/MC/V.

A perennial favorite and always crowded, the **Buena Vista Café** overlooks the cable car turntable in tiny Victorian Park from 2765 Hyde, at Beach St. (474–5044). Famous as the spot where Irish coffee, of Shannon Airport fame, was first served in America, it's also known to locals as a great spot for breakfast all day, and there are sandwiches, salads, and chef specials for lunch after 11 A.M. Give it a try only if the crowds of tourists are not three deep at the bar. Open daily, and no credit cards or reservations are accepted.

One block west of the BV stands Ghirardelli Square, from its opening in 1964 a giant success with San Franciscans and tourists alike. Created from the rambling and unlovely industrial buildings that housed the Ghirardelli spice and chocolate factory from the early 1900s until 1964, it is one of the most successful urban reclamation projects.

The mellowed warmth of the old Woolen Mill (1864) and the Cocoa, Chocolate, and Mustard buildings (1900–16) has been retained and enhanced with skylights, plazas, fountains, and landscaping. All it took was imagination and an initial investment of $10 million.

The square has lost none of its freshness or charm over the ensuing 20 years. Flowers in huge pots still change with the seasons, benches tempt you to sit a spell and enjoy the bay and the breeze, and the scent of chocolate hangs in the air as of old—the Ghirardelli Chocolate Manufactory still uses vintage equipment for demonstration purposes at the back of the ice cream parlour, and a giant chocolate bar has become a classic San Francisco souvenir.

In all, there are just under 80 places to enjoy spending money in Ghirardelli Square, among them several of the city's top restaurants and Maxwell's Plum, a lively Continental restaurant and disco bar.

Dining in Ghirardelli Square

If you haven't sampled Hungarian food, **Paprikás Fono** on the third level of the Cocoa Building is a grand place to begin. Although they probably can seat you without a long wait,

hold out for a table with a view in the glassed-in porch area,
the better to watch the tourists down below and the traffic
on the bay, especially at sunset (441–1223). The informal
decor is homespun Hungarian, with peasant designs on the
chairs and ceiling, and the house specialities include kettle-
cooked *gulyas* soup, *palacsintas* (a crepe with various fillings),
and chicken strudel (chicken cooked in paprika sauce,
chopped, rolled in thin strudel dough, and baked until crisp).
You also should order *langos,* a fried peasant bread that arrives at your table with half a clove of raw garlic. Whether
you rub it on the hot bread is up to you. Suffice to say that
the eau de garlic will outlast your day. Prices are moderate,
the dress is casual, and it's open for lunch and dinner daily
from 11:30 A.M. MC/V.

Tandoor—the art of cooking marinated foods in clay ovens
over white-hot charcoal—is the specialty of **Gaylord's,** a pol-
ished bit of India on the third floor of the Chocolate Building.
Meats, poultry, and chunks of seafood are marinated for
hours in special spices before being baked in the tandoori
ovens, and the result is outstanding—the fish tikka kabab and
tandoori chicken will live in memory. A glass wall in front
of the ovens lets you watch some of the process. The menu
goes far beyond curries in other ways, although the traditional chicken and lamb are offered. If you're adventurous, one
of the chef's special dinners will hit the high spots. You'll also
want to try one of the seven Indian breads baked on the sides
of the tandoori ovens, and *lassi,* an Indian drink of yogurt
and rose water made sweet or salty to your taste. The dining
room is nicely formal, with touches of Chippendale and Indian art. Lunch ranges from $10–$13.25; dinner from
$18–$24.50. Reservations are advised (771–8822). There is
a second Gaylord's, also highly recommended, in Embarcadero Center One (397–7775). AE/CB/DC/MC/V.

Awards on the wall at **The Mandarin,** on the fourth floor
of the Woolen Mill, are well earned, and you can buy owner
Cecilia Chiang's cookbook as you leave to find out why her
Peking-Shanghai-Szechuan food is so good. Five of the
world-class house specialties—Peking duck, beggar's chick-
en, shark's fin soup, Mongolian firepot, and stuffed cucumber
soup—must be ordered one day in advance, but the family
dinners for two or more ($20–$24 per person) are good imme-
diate selections. Two or three main dishes and rice, served

family-style, are recommended for lunch ($12–$14 per person). Although casual dress is fine here, the restaurant itself is elegant, with treasures salvaged from Mme. Chiang's former homes in Peking and Shanghai. Reservations are advised, but not always necessary, particularly after the summer tourist rush is over (673–8812 or 474–5438). AE/CB/DC/MC/V.

For good Mexican food in a great atmosphere, head for **Compadres Bar and Grill** on the second level of the Mustard Building. The outside deck overlooks both the square and the bay, and there are heaters to ward off the chills. Open daily for lunch and dinner (885–2266). AE/MC/V.

Dixie's Yacht Club Bar and Cafe, immediately left of the main entrance stairs to GS, is another great place for an alfresco lunch or to relax at the end of the day. Pick up their calendar of events; they sponsor goofy theme parties every Saturday night, and on "$2 Tuesday" all beer, wine, and well drinks are $2. Open daily from 11 A.M. to 1:30 A.M. (928–4733). AE/MC/V.

PIER 39

Many San Franciscans regard this 45-acre playland-on-the-pier as a crass and commercial upstart, but tourists love this latest addition to the Northern Waterfront scene. More than 12 million visitors come here yearly.

For generations an old cargo pier used for occasional shipping, Pier 39 was spruced up with a $54-million facelift and opened in 1978 as the rustic setting for 125 one-of-a-kind shops, 14 restaurants, and a 350-berth marina. One third of the buildings and the first and second level walkways are faced with weathered wood salvaged from the waterfront, and the ambience seems more Cape Cod than California Coast.

The fun possibilities are universal and almost endless. A $6 fee and a $25 deposit in cash or credit card get you a roll of film and let you borrow a Polaroid camera from Polaroid Expressions (956–4384) at the front of the pier to record your day. Daily performances on the three open-air stages include jugglers, magicians, musicians, and mimes year-round. You might also enjoy a ride on Mindscaper, which puts you in the front row of a roller coaster, on skis for a downhill race, or at the wheel of a racing car.

Kitemakers of San Francisco is here, should you want to shoot the breeze in Aquatic Park, along with shops devoted exclusively to cat-themed items, orange-crate label art, music boxes, scrimshaw, goodies for lefthanders, pig-inspired objects, butterfly-related accessories, handcrafted candles, and wooden puzzles.

Pier 39 shops are open daily from 10:30 A.M. to 8:30 P.M. (summer), 11 A.M. to 7:30 P.M. (winter). The eateries are open from 11:30 A.M. to 11:30 P.M. year-round, and they will validate for free parking in the Pier 39 garage after 6 P.M.

Dining

Tourists who stumble upon the **Eagle Café** (433–3689), on the top level (front) of Pier 39, may think they've passed through a time warp. No designer would create it or claim it, with its imitation wood floor, green formica tables, and mongrel mix of church basement chairs. An old wooden bar runs along the far side of the room, mute testimony to decades of dedicated elbow bending, and a remarkable collection of calendars, photos, fishing derby notices, sports schedules, "gimmee (novelty)" hats, and beer signs hangs on the walls. It looks like a hole-in-the-wall restaurant that belongs on the docks—and that's exactly what it was and still is.

The Eagle Café stood for many years on the corner of Powell and the Embarcadero, now the northwest corner of the Pier 39 garage. The question of whether to demolish it or preserve it as a historic place was a hot issue during the building of Pier 39, and ultimately it was jacked up, rolled down the street, and hoisted to its present site. A weathered, clapboard structure of uncertain lineage and vintage, it looks right at home, until you walk in the door.

Even the prices remind one of the good old days. The works at breakfast is $3.95; lunch ranges from about $2.25 (soup) to under $5 for the daily specials; and the bar starts setting 'em up at 7 A.M. with a top drink price of $4.25. The homemade cheesecake and chili have had devoted followings for years, and there's live music on Friday and Saturday nights. For a look at Embarcadero life before the days of plastic and tourist hype, drop in. Food is served weekdays from

6:30 A.M. to 2:30 P.M., weekends from 7 A.M. to 3 P.M.; the bar is open until 9:30 P.M. on weeknights, 2 A.M. on Friday and Saturday. No credit cards.

ON THE BAY

Enjoying San Francisco Bay is a breeze. Bring a picnic basket and set sail for the Golden Gate with skipper **John Tansley** on his Cal 28 sloop, $10 per person per hour (Pier 39, Dock A, Slip 1; 421–8353). Better yet, you can paddle your own sea kayak around the inlets and islands of the north bay. **Sea Trek Kayaking** in Sausalito offers that with no advance instruction required, as well as a three-hour introductory course ($45) that will allow you to go farther and faster. Basic rental price for a double kayak is $45 per person. (332–4457). MC/V.

Back in pre-bridge days, 50 ferries carried 50 million passengers a year across the waters of San Francisco Bay. Then the bridges opened, and what had been a tedious journey by boat became an easy commute by car. Slowly, the ferries died, the last one in the 1960s.

Today, the ferries are back in force—sleeker, swifter, and serving more destinations and people than ever before. The commuter ferries to Sausalito and Larkspur (332–6600) and to Tiburon (546–2815) dock at Pier One at the Ferry Building. Three firms offer an assortment of bay excursions from several piers along the Northern Waterfront. All are fun to ride, and a day at their destinations can be the highlight of your San Francisco trip. The following information was correct at presstime. Recheck before buying tickets.

The Red & White Fleet: The 45-minute *Bay Cruise* skirts the waterfront and skyline, loops under the Golden Gate, and passes Alcatraz. Scenic cruisers leave every 75 minutes from piers 41 and 43½ daily, starting at 10:45 A.M.; no reservations are necessary.

Escape to Alcatraz leaves Pier 41 every half hour from 8:15 A.M. June through October, 8:45 A.M. the rest of the year. You should arrive at the pier 20 minutes before sailing time and allow about 2½ hours for the total trip. For information, departure times, and fares, call 546–2896 or 800–445–8880 (California only). Tickets for weekends, holidays, and the summer season should be bought at least three weeks in advance, as this is the most popular trip of all. Alcatraz is part of the Golden Gate National Recreation Area, and you can rent an audiotape when you buy your ticket for a fascinating, self-guided tour. Expect to see the cells, mess hall, library, solitary-confinement section, and exercise yard of this former maximum security prison, as well as reminders of the American Indian occupation. Wear comfortable walking shoes and bring a sweater and camera—the views of the city are splendid.

An alternate *Alcatraz* cruise circles the rock twice in 45 minutes with an on-board narration by former prison guard Frank Heaney. Offered three times a week, it's ideal for those who find extended walking and touring too strenuous.

The *Angel Island/Fisherman's Wharf Ferry* has one morning departure daily from Pier 43½, with mid-afternoon returns. Four additional weekend departures are added in summer. This wooded island has a 740-acre wildlife preserve, small coves for picnicking, hiking and biking trails, and guided tram tours on weekends.

The *Marine World Africa USA Cruises* depart from Pier 41 on a 55-minute run to Vallejo and include bus transportation and admission to an outstanding mammal and wildlife park, a full day's outing. Picnics are advised; snack bars are the only other option. This trip operates Wednesday through Sunday in winter, daily in summer.

Just want to see more of the bay? Skip the marine park and ride the *Vallejo Ferry* round-trip. There are several departures daily, and the route includes Angel Island and the Ferry Building.

The *Sausalito/Tiburon/Fisherman's Wharf Ferry* has five departures daily from Pier 43½, with an additional evening run on weekends from March through September.

By reservation only, June through October (546–2803): *Golden Gate Sunset Cocktail Cruises* on weekday evenings, and a *dinner-dance cruise* on Friday evenings, all from Pier 41.

The Blue and Gold Fleet: The 75-minute *Bay Cruise* skirts the waterfront, passes under the Golden Gate and behind Alcatraz, and continues to the Bay Bridge before returning to its dock at Pier 39's west marina. Departures start at 10 A.M.

March through November; 11 A.M. December through February.

By reservation only: special *Barbecue on the Bay* cruises on Friday and Saturday nights from late April through October, also from Pier 39 (781–7890).

Hornblower Yachts: Weekday luncheon cruises, weekend brunch cruises, and nightly dinner-dance cruises are offered aboard either the *City of San Francisco* or the *Commodore Hornblower.* There are also special theme cruises throughout the year: Brazilian Night, Fiesta Alegre, Full Moon, Chinese New Year's, etc. All depart from Pier 33 (434–0300).

SAUSALITO

Exploring

Sausalito is a pleasant day's outing across San Francisco Bay, and getting there by ferry is half the fun. Bring some stale French bread to feed the gulls—they'll swoop down and peck from a loaf held in your hand—and then take a seat on the top deck for the best views. A jacket is advisable for this 20-minute trip in almost all seasons.

With some artistic license, this small, bay-front town has been described as the Portofino of California, a cascade of architecturally diverse homes down the hills, almost to the water. A single main street, Bridgeway, tucks along the edge of Richardson Bay, and the ferries dock in the heart of town. (If the weather isn't prime, you may prefer a guided coach tour to Sausalito or a drive over the Golden Gate Bridge yourself. Parking is tight, but not impossible.)

A low-key artist's colony a generation ago, Sausalito used to be a letdown to visitors expecting Carmel-type shopping and a fishing-village atmosphere. Things have changed, and first or return visits are definitely in order. A stroll south on El Portal from the ferry pier now passes expensive boutiques and the nicely refurbished Sausalito Hotel. If you're into "inns," take a look. Continuing south on Bridgeway, you'll pass a bronze sea lion rising from the bay, en route to three recommended restaurants: Angelino's, Ondine, and Horizons. The last-named is described in the Dining section below.

Heading north on Bridgeway from the ferry slip takes you into the heart of town. There are numerous flossy shops, and the four-level **Village Fair,** 777 Bridgeway, is the biggest tourist draw in Sausalito, with some 40 vendors selling things you never knew you wanted or needed.

Continuing north on the harbor side of the street, yachts soon give way to a large colony of unique houseboats or "arks." Created in the early 1960s by members of Sausalito's Bohemian art colony as alternatives to escalating rents ashore, these floating masterpieces periodically come under official scrutiny for zoning and health reasons. Yet they survive as part of the Sausalito scene and are fun to view.

Nearby at 2100 Bridgeway, you'll find a 47,000-square-foot working model of San Francisco Bay and its delta, built by Army engineers. Free and open from 9 A.M. to 5 P.M., Tuesday through Saturday, this interesting model reproduces, on a scale of 1:1,000, the rise and fall of the tides, flow and currents of water, sediment mixes, and other physical forces at work in the bay. The trip back on the ferry takes on new meaning.

Before you board the ferry, do two things. Make sure you are on the right boat (the red-and-white ones go to Fisherman's Wharf; the blue-and-white M/V *Golden Gate* goes to the Ferry Building), and buy some take-out fish and chips for a picnic on a bayside bench. Sailboats bright with spinnakers scud by, and Tiburon shimmers like Shangri-La across the bay—a perfect ending for a Sausalito day.

Dining

Horizon's, 558 Bridgeway (331-3232), makes the most of its site, the 1898 home of the San Francisco Yacht Club. The handcrafted wood interior is nice, with large windows looking out on the deck and beyond to the bays and San Francisco. Amazingly, some people prefer to eat inside on glorious days, when the deck seems one of the world's perfect spots. The food ranges from fresh seafood, milk-fed veal, steaks, and chicken to fresh salads, sandwiches, and assorted specials. Although tasty and well-presented, the meals are a tad pricier than similar offerings in the city, so a simple order of drinks and/or dessert may appeal. Brunch is a good bet too, served until 3 P.M. daily. The pace is leisurely, the dress is very casual, and reservations are advised. Open for lunch and dinner daily. MC/V.

If you want views and exercise, look for a long flight of steep steps above a small park on the west side of Bridgeway. A right turn on Josephine Street at the top of the stairs and a short walk brings you to a Sausalito landmark, the **Alta Mira Hotel.** If the weather is fine, lunch or brunch on the large, tree-top deck is memorable, and reservations are a necessity (332–1350). All of Sausalito and the bay lies before you, the best view in town. AE/CB/DC/MC/V.

From the hotel on Buckley Avenue, a narrow lane and steps lead back to Bridgeway. Directly opposite is Plaza Vina del Mar, a small park with a fountain and unusual elephant lamps from the 1915 Panama-Pacific Exposition, and to both left and right are several blocks of shops, eateries, etc. Two are worth watching for. The shoe-box size **Hamburgers,** 737 Bridgeway, draws lunch crowds daily. The **No Name Bar,** 757 Bridgeway, has no sign, but you'll have no trouble finding it. Discovered by the world after its cover was blown by an article in *Esquire,* this favored local hangout makes Ramos Fizzes and Bloody Marys from scratch and serves a variety of good coffee drinks as well. There's a small patio in back, and a pocket stage showcases local jazz and ragtime musicians on Thursday evenings and Sunday afternoons (332–1392). No credit cards.

Hotels

Long treasured as a French restaurant as well as a Victorian bed-and-breakfast lodging, **Casa Madrona Hotel and Restaurant,** 801 Bridgeway, now attracts the likes of James Farentino, Brooke Shields, and Harrison Ford with its 16 new units on the hillside adjacent to the Village Fair. Each room has been designed by a different decorator with cost being no object, and the results are spectacular—just about the best in the B&B business. Ranging from $125 to $300 a night, rooms include an airy artist's loft, complete with easel, paints, and brushes; the Renoir Room, with hand-painted fabrics on the walls and window seat, fireplace, elevated tub, and deck; and Lord Ashley's Lookout, a nineteenth-century retreat done in oak. Others follow Indian, Victorian, Oriental, Hollywood, and French themes, and a few are just indescribable or romantically fancy. Snoopers note: There's a room tour every afternoon at 2:30 and an album of room photos at the front desk. (801 Bridgeway, Sausalito, 94965; 415–332–0502.)

The original **Casa Madrona** could not be a greater contrast. Thirteen rooms ($80–$190) fill a grand Victorian home on top of the hill, built by a lumber baron in 1885. All have antiques and views, some have fireplaces, and all but two have private baths. Five cottages ($140–$160) follow their own themes on the spacious grounds.

All guests are welcome at the complimentary Continental breakfast served from 7:30 to 10 A.M. in the house dining room, which also is the Casa Madrona Restaurant. The restaurant also serves American nouvelle specialties from 6 to 10 P.M., Monday through Saturday, and hotel guests are given priority on reservations (331–5888). Dressy casual is fine for this candlelight-and-roses setting overlooking the bay. AE/MC/V.

FORT MASON

Formerly a military embarcation point, Fort Mason, at the Northern Waterfront, now is home to many community organizations and groups offering a variety of programs. To find out what's on today, call 441–5705. For additional or advance information, contact the GGNRA (Golden Gate National Recreation Area) Headquarters, Fort Mason, San Francisco 94123 (556–0560).

Don't miss the **Farallon Islands Expeditions,** offered Friday through Sunday, June through October. Sponsored by the nonprofit Oceanic Society through the Fort Mason Center, this boat trip is your chance to see dolphins, seals, humpback and gray whales, and an incredible variety of birds in their natural environments. The Farallones are a protected wildlife habitat 27 miles west of the Golden Gate, the largest bird sanctuary in America outside Alaska. The Oceanic Society is licensed to patrol the islands and is allowed to anchor in a secluded cove to observe the wildlife. You can come along.

Wouldn't know a cormorant from a pelican? You won't be alone. At least 90 percent of the participants in these trips are novices. The U.S. Coast Guard-approved *Nautilus* leaves the San Francisco Yacht Harbor in the Marina at 9 A.M. and returns at 5 P.M. Trained naturalists and researchers are aboard, and the specially designed craft also has video education programs in the lounge and two outside viewing platforms. Reservations (474–3385) should be made three weeks in advance (do call on the spur of the moment, however; they may have room), and the $48 fee (cash or AE/MC/V) gains you a detailed confirmation packet discussing every aspect of the trip. Tea and coffee are gratis, but bring your own lunch.

The Oceanic Society also runs whale-watching trips aboard the 80-foot *Nautilus II* Friday through Monday during the migration season, December through mid-April. These 6½-hour trips are $34–$38 and also leave from the Marina on a run to Point Reyes off the Marin County coast. Please, no children under 10, no picnic baskets or coolers, and no high heels or open-toe shoes.

Fort Mason has five art galleries, including one in the unusual **Mexican Museum,** Building D. The museum's permanent collection includes outstanding folk art, lacquer ware, masks, and pre-Hispanic pieces from Jalisco and Colima. Admission $1; open from noon to 5 P.M., Wednesday through Sunday (441–0404). Look also for the **San Francisco Crafts and Folk Art Museum** in Building A, free and open afternoons except Monday (775–0990); the **Media Alliance** in Building D; the **World Print Gallery** in Building A; and the **Perception Gallery** in Building C.

If you're into avant-garde drama, check the playbill at the award-winning **Magic Theatre,** Building D, now in its 17th season of producing new plays by established and new playwrights (441–8822).

Maritime history buffs: the World War II liberty ship *Jeremiah O'Brien* is moored at Pier 3 of Fort Mason and open to visitors daily (441–3101).

Dining

Greens, in Building A, Fort Mason, is a typical San Francisco–style success story. Who would have guessed that a vegetarian restaurant opened by nonprofessionals in a cavernous and ugly shed, well out of the downtown area, would become one of the hottest places in town?

Certainly not the Zen Buddhists who started the place. Although reservations are no longer essential, do call well in advance for prime-time tables. Otherwise, take your chances at the last minute.

Combining a flair for seasoning with a respect for very fresh food, the staff creates extraordinary soups, salads, and entrées that have earned reams of plaudits from carnivorous reviewers and patrons. More than half who dine here are not vegetarians!

All the basic materials are fresh, some of them grown on the Buddhists' Green Gulch Farm in Marin County, and selected wines complement the food. The imaginative breads come from another Zen enterprise, the Tassajara Bread Bakery, which also has a take-out counter.

And don't think you'll be dining in a warehouse. One wall is all windows and looks out on the Marina yacht harbor and the Golden Gate, and a giant redwood sculpture dominates the far end of the room. It is light, airy, and a grand relief from the engineered elegance of more conventional restaurants.

Lunch and dinner are served Tuesday through Saturday; call early in the week for Sunday brunch reservations (771–6222). Beer and wine only. The Tassajara bread is sold from 9:30 A.M. to 4:30 P.M., Tuesday through Saturday. MC/V.

PALACE OF FINE ARTS

From Fort Mason, it's an easy stroll to the **Marina Green,** the next link of the Golden Gate Promenade. This is a good place for a picnic (see the Dining chapter) and to watch the boat traffic in and out of the St. Francis Yacht Club. You also can try one of the city's two Parcourses here, a jogging and exercise circuit popular with physical-fitness enthusiasts making their daily trek from Aquatic Park to Fort Point.

Although not a part of the GGNRA, the nearby **Palace of Fine Arts** is another grand people place. It was designed by famed architect Bernard Maybeck as one of 32 impermanent plaster "palaces" for the 1915 Panama-Pacific International Exhibition. Too handsome to tear down with the others, this facsimile of a Roman ruin and its rotunda crumbled

into a real ruin over the ensuing decades. Community outcry
brought about its $8 million reconstruction in the early 1960s,
and today it adds the feel of Rome and the beauty of Paris
to the city. The surrounding park is a perfect picnic site, and
the palace building now houses the **Exploratorium** (3601
Lyon St. at Marina Blvd.).

This hands-on museum lets you manipulate exhibits on
natural and scientific phenomena. The museum shop continues the theme and is worth a visit itself. Open 1 to 5 P.M.,
Thursday and Friday; 1 to 9:30 P.M. on Wednesday; and 10
A.M. to 5 P.M. on weekends. Admission ($4.50) is free on the first
Wednesday of the month and every Wednesday evening
(563–7337).

GOLDEN GATE BRIDGE

Who can resist the opportunity to walk over the Pacific and
back? The wide pedestrian walkways of the Golden Gate
Bridge let you do just that, a 3½-mile total jaunt. Take your
camera—shots of the city to the east are best in the afternoon—and be prepared to feel the pulse of the bridge under
your feet. Looking down on passing ships is no small thrill
either. Access is from the Golden Gate Promenade on foot,
or via Muni Bus No. 28 from Fisherman's Wharf and Fort
Mason to the bridge toll plaza.

Tucked under the south ramparts of the bridge is a piece
of the city's past, **Fort Point National Historic Site**
(556–1693). This massive red-brick fortification was built between 1853–61 by the U.S. Army Corps of Engineers to pro-
tect the mouth of the bay. Now, as a museum within the
GGNRA, it offers visitors a chance to relive those Civil War
days with tours by the National Park staff, daily from 10 A.M.
to 5 P.M. The outside dike is a favorite spot for late afternoon
fishing. Stop and check out the day's catch.

The coastal trail along the west side of the Presidio is
reached by the No. 29 Muni bus, just in case you feel like
a hike. The trail ends at **Baker Beach,** a long strand great
for sunning or strolling, but *not* for swimming. On weekends
park rangers demonstrate the "disappearing" gun, a 95,000-
pound cannon in Battery Chamberlain behind the beach. The
rest of the Presidio's 1,698 acres is best covered by car.

Pacific Heights

Exploring

Exploring Pacific Heights is one of San Francisco's surprising pleasures. The area bounded by Lombard Street, Van Ness Avenue, California Street, and Presidio Avenue has been the high-rent district for generations.

As a result, you'll find handsome Painted Ladies here— grand Victorian houses to see and tour—as well as excellent shopping and dining on both Union and Sacramento streets. Viewing by car is easy, thanks to a tour map from the San Francisco Convention & Visitors Bureau. However, some of the suggested 6½-mile tour route is in the dangerous Western Addition, so take precautions. You will want to stop in the late afternoon to photograph the **Painted Ladies of Alamo Square** (712–722 Steiner), backed by the towers of the Financial District.

The best way to appreciate these technicolor relics is to stroll the blocks around Lafayette Square and Alta Plaza Park with an educated eye. Basically, there are four styles. The earliest is 1850–70s Italianate, identified by a flat roof (sometimes hidden behind a false front), slim or Corinthian pillars by the front door, narrow windows, and bays with either slanted or narrow side windows. The Stick style added wood outline to the doors, frame, and bay windows of the Italianate house, and the Stick/Eastlake (1880s) tacked on the gingerbread. The Queen Anne (1890s) has turrets, towers, a steep and gabled roof, and often sections of shingle siding somewhere.

Now you are ready to tour on your own or enjoy Heritage Walks (441–3004). These guided tours ($3) of houses in the eastern Pacific Heights neighborhood leave every Sunday at 12:30 P.M. from the **Haas-Lilienthal House,** 2007 Franklin.

This handsome 1886 mansion is a great place to start. A mix of the Stick and Queen Anne styles, it still has most of the family furnishings in its 22 rooms and is owned by The Foundation for San Francisco's Architectural Heritage. Guided tours ($3) are given every Wednesday from noon to 4 P.M. and Sunday from 11 A.M. to 4:30 P.M. (441–3004).

Next stop is the elegant 1894 **Whittier Mansion** at 2090 Jackson St. (567–1848), now the headquarters for the California Historical Society and open for viewing on Wednesday, Saturday, and Sunday, with tours at 1:30 and 3 P.M. Admission is $2 adult, $1 for senior citizens and children. Several blocks away at Gough (pronounced "Goff") and Union is **Octagon House,** built in 1861 and one of the two such homes remaining in the city. Owned by the National Society of Colonial Dames, it is open on the second Sunday and second and fourth Thursdays of the month from noon to 3 P.M. (441–7512). Donation required. Closed January.

Although the following are not open to the public, they are worth seeing from the sidewalk: The Willis Polk-designed Georgian brick mansion at 2550 Webster; the Italian Renaissance palace at 2222 Broadway and its neighbor (2220), now the property of the Convent of the Sacred Heart; and the Adolph Spreckels home at 2080 Washington. Also walk along the 2000 block of Gough; the 2000–2200 blocks of Pine; and the 1700–2200 blocks of California. Nos. 1911–21 on Sacra-

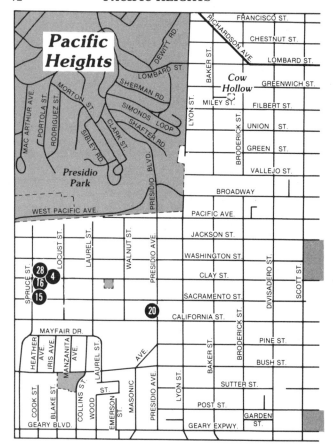

Points of Interest

1) To Alamo Square, Painted Ladies
2) Balboa Cafe
3) Bed & Breakfast Inn
4) Beyond Expectations
5) Chelsea Motor Inn
6) Coffee Cantata
7) Blue Light Cafe
8) Pierce St. Annex
9) Doidge's Kitchen
10) The Majestic
11) Haas-Lilienthal House
12) Italianate Row Houses
13) Italian Renaissance Palace
14) La Petite Boulangerie
15) Mark Twain Court (3600 block)
16) Mary Gulli's Restaurant

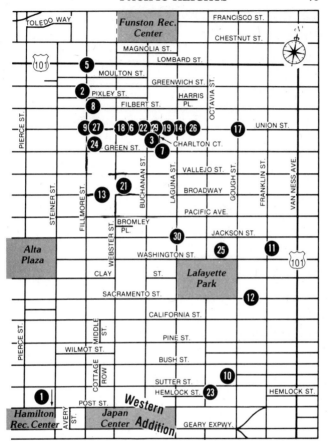

17) Octagon House
18) Original Farm House
    with Barn
19) Perry's
20) Picnix
21) Polk's Georgian Brick
    Mansion
22) Prego
23) Queen Anne Hotel
24) Shorman House

25) Spreckels Mansion
26) Stable Facing
    Washerman's Lagoon
27) Tarr & Feathers
28) Tuba Garden Restaurant
29) Victorian Wedding Houses
30) Whitter Mansion

mento are four Italianate row houses that are also worth viewing.

Hotels

A number of the Pacific Heights Victorian homes also accept overnight guests, among them the Queen Anne Hotel, the Bed and Breakfast Inn, and Sherman House.

Although technically in the Western Addition area of town, the **Queen Anne Hotel** prefers to say it is a European-style guest house in lower Pacific Heights. Either way, the neighborhood remains acceptable at this writing (two blocks south of Pacific Heights and two blocks east of Japantown), and the hotel is a gem. A fresh and handsome restoration of an 1890s school for young ladies, it has 49 good-sized rooms with baths, soundproofing, oversized beds, and most of the amenities you would expect in a luxury hotel. A Continental breakfast, either in the dining room or in bed, is included, along with afternoon tea and sherry downstairs with the other guests from 4 to 6 P.M. Rooms are $89–$139. (1590 Sutter St., San Francisco 94109; 415–441–2828; 800–262–2663 in CA; 800–227–3970 elsewhere.)

One of SF's grandest hotels when it was built in 1902, the **Majestic** again gleams after a costly restoration. All 60 rooms have either four-poster or canopied beds, private baths, and heavy lace curtains, many have fireplaces. The Cafe Majestic, making waves in SF's restaurant scene, serves breakfast, lunch, and dinner. Rates are $95 single, $115–$160 double, $160 for suites. (1500 Sutter at Gough, San Francisco 94109; 415–441–1100; 800–824–0094 in CA; 800–252–1155 elsewhere.)

Two small Italianate buildings (1873–1896) in a small court off Union Street house the **Bed and Breakfast Inn,** the first of its kind in San Francisco when it opened in 1976. Each of eight rooms and a private flat are individually furnished with cozy flair, the perfect place for a romantic interlude. Many of the furnishings are family antiques, others are bright contemporary pieces, and the combination is so nice you won't want to leave, even to prowl Union Street.

The main house at Four Charlton Court has a library and breakfast area, although breakfast in bed is the general rule. Upstairs are four pension rooms that share facilities

($68–$85). The second house at Two Charlton has four suites ($114–$129), with private baths—"Celebration" has a sunken double bathtub—and the "Mayfair" above the main house is a luxurious three-room flat with latticed balcony and a spiral staircase to the bedroom loft ($184). Five Charlton is a cozy double with a single bed in a sleeping alcove (no children under 10) and a tiny kitchenette ($108). Reservations are suggested two to three months in advance and no credit cards are accepted. (Four Charlton Court, San Francisco 94123; 415–921–9784.)

It's easy to find **Sherman House,** SF's newest small luxury hotel. Just look for the Bentley, Daimler, or Silver Shadow limo in the drive of a gleaming, vintage mansion on Green Street. Its 10 rooms and five suites attract all manner of blue-chip folk who gladly pay the $170–$600 a day tariff. Each room is furnished to *haute luxe,* the private restaurant is superb, and for an extra fee you'll be met at the airport with one of those vintage limos. The Leander Sherman Suite's giant terrace overlooks all the bay, and Bjorn Borg hid away in the Garden Suite with its two private courtyards. (2160 Green St., San Francisco 94123; 415–563–3600.)

UNION STREET

Exploring and Shopping

This is the hottest retail street in town, and things change very swiftly. Every month sees the opening of a new specialty shop or restaurant in the eight blocks between Van Ness Avenue and Steiner Street. There is very little here one truly needs, but everything one could want.

Long known as Cow Hollow because of its bucolic use a century ago, **Union Street** developed in the Victorian era. Then, through the mid-1950s, it was a low-key business and service area for the carriage trade of upper Pacific Heights. The showcase potential of its Victorians was then discovered, and as a shopping area it has moved from being charming and low key to contrived and pricey.

But it is still fun. This is where the action is, day and night—and even on Sunday afternoons. Neighboring Filbert Street is blossoming too—there are only so many Victorians to tart up on Union—so you'll want to stroll there and on the side streets also.

Among the possible finds: wine-tasting bars, live mannequins posing among the dummies in the window of Janice Lee boutique, flower stands on the sidewalks, super slices of pie at Bepples, quick snacks at Out to Lunch. Hankering for breakfast? Try **Doidge's Kitchen,** 2217 Union (921–2149). The atmosphere is casual, the service very good, the coffee top-notch, and the corned-beef hash exceptional—made with mushrooms, it's not at all greasy.

Union Street and environs are classy singles territory. Two of the best places are the **Balboa Café,** at 3199 Fillmore (922–4595), and the **Pierce St. Annex,** at 3138 Fillmore (567–1400), a favorite with laid-back locals. But **Perry's,** 1944 Union (922–9022), draws everyone, every evening. Good food is served in the back dining room, if you ever get past the bar. Some consider Perry's the premier pickup bar of San Francisco, so polish your technique if you're on the prowl. The young hoot-and-holler crowd tops off the evening with live music and entertainment at **Tarr and Feathers,** 2140 Union (563–2612).

Dining

Boz Scaggs's **Blue Light Cafe,** across from Perry's at 1979 Union (922–5510), is the latest entry in the Union Street singles scene. Open daily from 4 P.M. to 2 A.M., this is a good spot to meet and mix while filling up on Tex-Mex-style food. House specials range from a fajitas sandwich you build yourself in a giant flour tortilla to mesquite-grilled chicken, ribs, and a variety of fresh fish. Boz drops in periodically, and taped Motown sounds from the sixties back up the chitchat. This unpretentious place is popular with the under-40 smart set, and evening reservations are a necessity. MC/V.

Coffee Cantata, 2030 Union (931–0770), is a favorite with the 35-and-over set, a coffeehouse set to opera music. There's good dining up in back, but the action, particularly from 5 to 7 P.M., is at the tables in front by the bar. This also is a meeting place, but even shy singles are comfortable here. The food offerings are light eclectic, everything from pastas, dolmas, and beef stew to chicken in assorted disguises. You can also get hot and cold sandwiches as well as a variety of ice-cream drinks and desserts until midnight. Open daily for lunch and dinner, and prices are moderate. AE/MC/V.

Prego is next door at 2000 Union (563–3305) and is considered by many the hottest restaurant in town. A gathering spot disguised as an Italian trattoria, the place is hardly visible through the crowd. One of the three dining rooms has a skylight with an outside herb garden around it, the better to flavor the pizzas cooked in huge, oakwood ovens. Another favorite is a *toasti,* the Italian version of a grilled ham and cheese sandwich served at the bar. The food is fresh, the pasta is memorable, and the prices are great ($4.95–$15.95). You can solve the world's problems here without being hustled for your table. They expect you to linger, and they offer magazines on library poles so you can look occupied and/or purposeful if you are by yourself. And if you're not interested in the straight-bore bar, try a *limonata,* a mix of fresh lemonade and mineral water served in a giant, frosted glass. Reservations are accepted for parties of six or more. Open daily for lunch and dinner. AE/DC/MC/V.

Hotels

For comfortable motel lodgings, the **Chelsea Motor Inn** at the corner of Fillmore and Lombard is a good choice. The spacious rooms are soundproof and have bay windows, and there's inside parking with good security just three blocks from the Union Street action. Rates are $67 single, $72 double. (2095 Lombard, San Francisco 94123; 415–563–5600). Should you prefer Laura Ashley–style cosseting and chocolates on your pillow at night, reserve at the **Marina Inn Bed and Breakfast,** 3110 Octavia (at Lombard), San Francisco 94123; 415–938–1000). Victorian in style, this charming inn includes a Continental breakfast and afternoon sherry in its $55–$75 single or double room rate.

SACRAMENTO STREET

Exploring

Sacramento Street, between Spruce and Baker streets, is also good for strolling. Dotted with shops and small restaurants, it still belongs to its neighborhood rather than to the tourists and swingers. Don't miss the lane into charming **Mark Twain Court** in the 3600 block. Tucked away here are shops selling art, bonsai, and Chinese antiques, as well as one of the street's best spots for lunch.

Dining

Mary Gulli's Restaurant, 3661 Sacramento, is that rarity, a small, chef-owned haven dedicated to good food. A refined brown-and-beige restoration in an old carriage house in Mark Twain Court, Mary Gulli's is a favorite of Pacific Heights's well-dressed Upper Crust. The menu is eclectic, and your best bets are the inspired daily specials. You can sit in the flower-trimmed outdoor courtyard, weather permitting. Dress up for this, and call for reservations (931–5151). Lunch is served from 11:45 A.M. to 3 P.M. and dinner from 6 to 9 P.M. Tuesday through Thursday, until 10 P.M. Friday and Saturday. AE/MC/V.

Across the way at 3634 Sacramento is the **Tuba Garden Restaurant,** fun for lunch or brunch in its brick-walled garden. While you devour your delicious salad, quiche, or soup, search for the giant tuba stuck up in the ivy for comic relief. Open daily. Reservations are advised (921–TUBA). AE/CB/DC/MC/V.

The Magic Flute, opposite at 3673 Sacramento, specializes in fresh food cooked with as little salt and saturated fat as possible. There's an Italian slant to the weekly menu and another outdoor courtyard here. Open weekdays for lunch, nightly for dinner. Reservations suggested (922–1225). Both the Tuba Garden Restaurant and The Magic Flute also are art galleries. AE/CB/DC/MC/V.

If you are out early or want a quick lunch, **Beyond Expectations,** 3613 Sacramento, is a good bet. This small café/bakery prepares great food from scratch. The morning cheese pie with blueberries may revolutionize your breakfast habits, and the turkey pot pies have a fame all their own. There's a full espresso bar and fresh juices as well. Tables are in the back, and the daily papers make the rounds. If you give them a call in advance, they'll fix to-go orders. Open weekdays 8:30 A.M. to 5:30 P.M.; Saturday 9 A.M. to 5 P.M.; Sunday 10 A.M. to 3 P.M. (567–8640). No credit cards.

JAPANTOWN

Exploring

Bounded by Geary, Fillmore, Bush, and Laguna streets, the three square blocks of Japantown are the heart of a community established after the earthquake (1906) and the present home of an estimated 13,000 Japanese. Unfortunately, a Japanese style of architecture never flourished here, and the neighborhood remains an odd mix of restored or modernized Victorians and other nondescript styles. Only one section, the Buchanan Mall, fits the ethnic theme. This block-long stone street is lined with Japanese village-style buildings and highlighted by two unusual walk-in, sit-down fountains by Japanese sculptress Ruth Asawa. Buchanan Mall ends at Post and frames the futuristic Peace Pagoda across the street, the focal point of the massive **Japan Center.**

Built in 1968, this multimillion-dollar complex spreads over five acres and is experiencing both a physical and commercial rejuvenation. New shops are opening, so save time to wander. If you are in town during the Cherry Blossom Festival the last two weekends of April or the Aki Matsuri Festival in late September, it's a must. There are several other interesting celebrations over the year. If you are interested, check posters for current events as you walk around.

Put the Japan Center on your serious shopping list. In the West Building is **Ma-Shi-Ko Folk Craft,** great for browsing, with its stacks of Oriental art and antiques. They also sell the unusual Mashiko stoneware, based on 700-year-old designs. If you've been looking for an antique temple bell, this is the place. Nearby is **Shige Nishiguchi,** selling beautiful silk and cotton kimonos, many in unusual designs. This shop also specializes in obis (Japanese sashes) and fine Japanese collectibles, including antique dolls.

Kabuki Hot Spring, entered at 1750 Geary Blvd., will introduce you to the pleasures of the Japanese bath. The Sakura Plan (bath only) is $8; the Fuji Plan (bath and Shiatsu massage) is $25; and the one-hour Kabuki Plan (private bath, shower, sauna or steam, and Shiatsu massage) is $35. The first two are for women only on Wednesday and Sunday and for men only the rest of the week. The Kabuki Plan, however, is for either men or women at any time (separate rooms) and requires reservations (922–6002). The facilities are immaculate.

San Francisco's newest extravaganza for the senses, **The Duquette Pavilion of St. Francis,** is nearby at 1839 Geary. Called a "celebrational environment" by its artist-creator Tony Duquette, it's a glorious mix of archangels, tapestries, computer-controlled lighting, and skin-tingling sound. Open Wednesday–Sunday, 11 A.M. to 4 P.M. Admission is $4 (563–7341).

Hotels

Sleek after a $10-million renovation, the **Miyako Hotel** is an interesting place to stay. Guests are greeted by a kimono-clad Japanese lady at the foyer, and the guest rooms all have Japanese touches like sliding shoji screens over the windows. Twelve suites and two rooms have private saunas, and two suites and two rooms are classically Japanese, from the traditional futons on the tatami-mat floors to the sunken-tub baths. Not to worry; the Oriental bathrooms come with instructions for first-time Occidental visitors. The hotel's dining room is an outstanding alternative to the sushi bars and mysterious Oriental cuisine common to the neighborhood. The Sunday buffet ($19.50) is lavish, very eclectic, and Continental. Rooms are $95–$125, single or double; the higher the room, the higher the price. Japanese rooms are $125–$155, and the Japanese suite is $195. (1625 Post, San Francisco 94115; 922–3200, 800–533–4567.)

The Golden Gate
Park Area

Exploring

Rain or shine, there's fun to be found in Golden Gate Park. This 1,017-acre playground is half a mile wide and stretches inland 3.3 miles from the Great Highway along Ocean Beach to the center of metro San Francisco. Although it is easily reached by assorted Muni buses, you may want to have a car to cover the entire park, adjacent portions of the Golden Gateway National Recreation Area, and the San Francisco Zoo. There also are good restaurants to discover in these outlying districts.

The John F. Kennedy Drive entrance to the park from Fell Street passes the **Victorian Conservatory,** modeled after Kew Gardens in London and ablaze with flowers in every season.

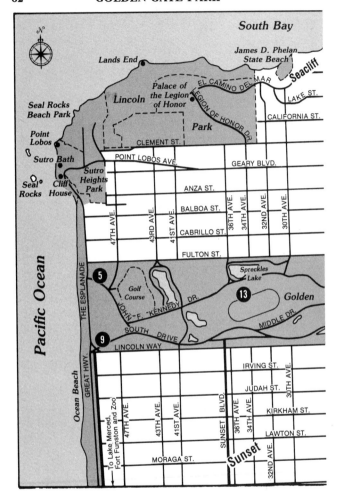

Points of Interest

1) Asian Art Museum
2) California Academy of Sciences

3) Conservatory
4) De Young Museum
5) Dutch Windmill
6) Japanese Tea Garden
7) Kezar Stadium & Pavilion

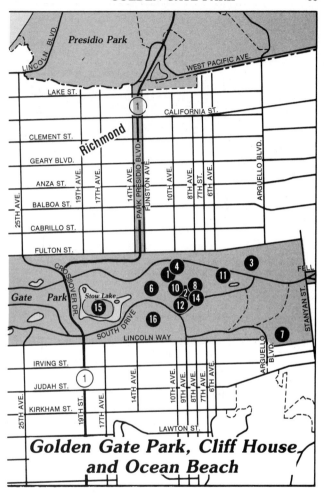

Golden Gate Park, Cliff House and Ocean Beach

8) Morrison Planetarium
9) Murphy Windmill
10) Music Concourse
11) Rhododendron Dell
12) Shakespeare Garden

13) Stables
14) Steinhart Aquarium
15) Strawberry Hill
16) Strybing Arboretum

This fanciful glass-domed greenhouse came around the horn on a sailing ship in the 1870s—stop in for the full story. In April and May, don't miss the nearby John McLaren Memorial **Rhododendron Dell,** 20 acres of beauty dedicated to the man who created Golden Gate Park from a wasteland of sand dunes.

The next left turn leads to the **Music Concourse,** site of the Mid-Winter Fair in 1894 and the heart of the park's activity zone today. Here you'll find the de Young and Asian museums of art across a large ground from the California Academy of Sciences. The latter houses an outstanding museum, aquarium, and natural-science museum—interesting anytime, but great refuges on a rainy day. On nice-weather weekends, there are often open-air concerts in the concourse bandshell, and picnics abound. Behind the Academy of Sciences is the tiny Garden of Shakespeare's Flowers, planted exclusively with 200 blossoms identified by quotations from his writings.

The Asian museum is flanked by the incomparable **Japanese Tea Garden,** five acres of enchantment created in 1894 for the Mid-Winter Fair. The pleasures of this delicate reserve are ruined by crowds; pass on if there are tour buses parked outside. Early mornings and late afternoons are particularly nice. Admission is free from 8 to 9 A.M. and 5 to 7 P.M., and the sense of serenity is unmatched. Don't miss the teahouse, where a kimono-clad Japanese lady will serve you jasmine or green tea with a tray of cookies. The cherry trees bloom here in April, and their fragile beauty lasts for several weeks as the blossoms fall in a rain of petals.

A short walk behind the garden leads to **Stowe Lake,** another great place for picnics and strolling. Rowboats, motor boats, and peddle boats can be rented here ($8.50–$11 per hour) daily (except Mondays) year-round, weather permitting (752–0347). With a picnic, this is a nice place to while away an afternoon. The new Golden Gate Pavilion, a gift from San Francisco's sister city of Taipei, marks Strawberry Hill Island in mid-lake.

A horse-drawn carriage ride is a fun way to help you get your bearings. The pick-up point is outside the Asian Art Museum, and the tour ($5–$15, at last notice, for up to three adults) comes in three sizes: the concourse, the conservatory, or Stowe Lake. MC/V.

The two museums are a day in themselves. The **M.H. de Young Memorial Museum** has 64 galleries around a central court, showing an extensive collection that spans the history of civilization. The gallery of Oceanic, African, and American art has audio recordings, and the east wing houses major international exhibitions. The Café de Young is an indoor-outdoor treat for lunch, highly recommended. The museum is open Wednesday through Sunday, 10 A.M. to 5 P.M.; the café is open only to 4 P.M. on those days. Admission is $4, free on Saturday mornings and the first Wednesday of the month. Free tours are given daily. No credit cards. (750–3600.)

The **Asian Art Museum** is next door, showcasing the Avery Brundage Collection of Oriental Arts. Docent tours are strongly recommended (668–8922); closed Monday and Tuesday.

You'll find art of another realm at the **Cosmic Laser Concerts** Wednesday through Sunday evenings at Morrison Planetarium. A krypton gas laser dances intricate patterns of light across the sky dome to the music of the Beatles, John Williams, Pink Floyd, Moon Rocks, Rainbow Cadenza, *Star Wars,* etc., and the effect is spectacular. Tickets ($3.50–$5.50) can be bought in advance through Ticketron (392–SHOW) or at the California Academy of Sciences half an hour before showtime (750–7138).

The music concourse connects Kennedy Drive with South Drive, which loops around **Strybing Arboretum,** a favorite jogging spot. Other beautiful gardens are scattered throughout the park. Don't miss the **Queen Wilhelmina Tulip Garden,** flanking the newly restored Dutch Windmill at the junction of Kennedy Drive with the Great Highway. The park also has a 1912 Hershel-Spillman carousel in the Children's Playground near Kezar Stadium, and a buffalo paddock is designed to look like an open range in the old west.

You don't have to walk or drive through the park. You'll find bicycles and roller skates for rent in the 600–800 blocks of Stanyan Street on the park's eastern border. Good news: the park is closed to traffic on Sunday; it's a skating and biking heaven. Also, the city recreation department maintains two bikeways. One passes through Golden Gate Park to Lake Merced; the other winds from the south end of town and crosses the Golden Gate Bridge into Marin County. Bike maps are available at McLaren Lodge, Fell and Stanyan streets, at the Kennedy Drive entrance to the park.

One-timers are welcome to take group or semiprivate riding lessons at **Golden Gate Stables,** Kennedy Drive and 34th Ave. (668–7360). Rates range from $12 to $17, and dressage is the house specialty. Although 27 miles of bridle paths thread the park, no trail rides are operating as of this writing due to high insurance costs.

Hotels

Two bed-and-breakfast accommodations in this area are well done, but they're advised only for those with a car.

The **Victorian Inn on the Park** looks out on runner's heaven, the panhandle of Golden Gate Park, and is proving popular with the jogging crowd as well as with couples wanting a romantic lodging. Built in 1897, this Queen Anne Victorian was designed by William Curtlett, whose other local claims to fame include the Phelan Building and the city hall. After some sad years, this mansion has been completely renovated, brought up to code, and now is an official historic landmark. It also is a nice place to stay—12 rooms with baths, antiques, good linens, queen-size beds, and nice touches like down pillows and fresh flowers ($75–$125). Two suites have park views and are a bit more pricey ($125–$225). Guests mingle in the late afternoon over sherry and wine in the downstairs parlor and library, and there's sherry in every room. Breakfast includes the morning paper, freshly ground and brewed coffee, fruit and juice, and croissants or freshly baked breads. The neighborhood is in transition but looking up. However, this is on the edge of the Western Addition and within the mixed Haight-Ashbury district, so street caution is advised. 301 Lyon, at Fell, San Francisco 94117; 415–931–1830.

More elaborate, **The Spreckles Mansion** is a bed-and-breakfast fantasy of rooms and suites high on Buena Vista Hill. Built in 1887, it has been decorated by masters. With the Guest House next door, built in 1897, there are ten lodgings, and staying in any one of them would be an only-in-San Francisco experience. The San Francisco Suite ($190, one couple; $290, two couples) covers the entire third floor, the mansion's former ballroom. The Star-Gazer Suite ($185) has a skylight over the bed, The Sunset Suite ($138) has a pair of canopied double beds and antique French etched windows, and the Sugar Baron Suite ($185) has a canopied bed alcove, Corinthian columns, and an enormous bathroom with a free-standing claw-foot tub in front of a fireplace. All have fine antiques, marvelous windows, designer linens—almost an overdose of delightful things. The two least expensive rooms ($88 and $98) share a bath but come with complimentary terry robes, so you won't have to scurry down the hall in your trench coat. 737 Buena Vista West, San Francisco 94117; 415–861–3008.

Dining

The **Ironwood Café,** 901 Cole (664–0224), has a citywide reputation for its fresh fish and chicken dishes as well as its tasty salads. The bent is California/American, and the menus change daily. Open weekdays for lunch; Monday through Saturday for dinner. Reservations advised. AE/MC/V.

Dish, at 1398 Haight (431–3534), is another good choice, particularly if your time, budget, and appetite are limited. Even the burgers are special here, along with omelets and entrees of the day. Breakfast is served until 1 P.M. daily; dinner nightly. AE/CB/MC/V.

If you stroll Haight Street, drop in at 1605 for a raspberry tart and coffee at the **Bakers of Paris.** Another of the small, new bakeries that are changing SF's French bread scene, this friendly place is open daily from 7:30 A.M. to 7 P.M. and has coffee to go.

CLIFF HOUSE

Exploring

The western end of Golden Gate Park fronts on the Great Highway and Ocean Beach, part of the Golden Gate National Recreation Area (GGNRA). Though too treacherous and cold for swimming, this four-mile shore offers exhilarating walks and jogs. North of Golden Gate Park, the Great Highway leads to Cliff House, Seal Rocks, Land's End, and China Beach. All are part of the GGNRA and fun to explore.

There has been a Cliff House on this site since 1863, and lunch here is a tradition. Your best bets are Upstairs at the Cliff House (soups/salads/omelets/sandwiches) and Phineas T. Barnacle (sandwich-and-salad deli/full-service bar). A window table at the latter looks out at Seal Rocks, a protected habitat not for seals, but for sea lions. The lower level of Cliff House has an observation deck with telescopes, the National Park Service office with wonderful photos of the old Sutro Baths, and the Musée Mechanique. Here you'll find all kinds of arcade machines from Victorian peep shows to video games. A quarter plays an old music box or lets you see Naughty Marietta sunbathing in the 3-D realism of six decades ago. Leonardo da Vinci's Camera Obscura is around the corner.

Next to Cliff House are the foundations of the old Sutro Baths, all that remains of a fantastic Victorian edifice that shared this headland from 1896 to the 1960's. A short walking path behind the ruins leads to Point Lobos, so named in 1769 by members of the Portola Expedition as they passed by. The highway continues along the coast to West Fort Miley, where you'll find walking trails along the edge of the coast to Land's End. The churning waters here are among the most treacherous in the world, and on a clear day you'll see the Farallon Islands to the west and Point Reyes to the north. The view is well worth the hike.

From the Cliff House environs, take Clement Street east to a left turn on El Camino Del Mar. After winding through Lincoln Park, you'll arrive at the magnificent **Palace of the Legion of Honor,** a museum devoted to the art and culture of France. Note the four massive sculptures outside and the views of the Golden Gate and the city. The museum's Café Chanticleer is a treat at lunch. (No credit cards, please.) Like the de Young, this museum is open Wednesday through Sunday, and docent tours are available (221–4811). A one-day admission ticket ($4) is good at all three major museums.

From the western side of the museum's parking lot, El Camino Del Mar continues along the coast into the expensive Seacliff residential area. A bearing to the left will bring you to the parking area for GGNRA's **China Beach** (also known as James D. Phelan Beach). This is one of the few swimming beaches in the city, and lifeguards are on duty during the summer months (556–7894).

Dining

There are many new and good restaurants on Geary Boulevard, Balboa Avenue, and Clement Street, in the Richmond District north of Golden Gate Park. The last is the most interesting—the city's "new" Chinatown—and is worth a stroll as well. Be warned that although these three streets parallel each other, the 100 blocks of Clement and Balboa coincide with the 3800 block of Geary, nice to know before you wander off the track.

You'll find ethnic foods you didn't even know existed in this district—block after block of Jewish delis next to Persian cafes next to Korean barbecues. One of the nicest and most gentle introductions to such culinary exotica comes at **Angkor Wat,** 4217 Geary. The atmosphere may be simple and subdued, but the Cambodian food definitely is not. Often spicy, it always is well-prepared here, a good choice for a special meal. Open for dinner only, Tuesday through Sunday (221–7887). AE/MC/V.

Less fancy and somewhat less expensive, **Cambodia House,** 5625 Geary, is another good choice for Cambodian food. Locals come from as far away as Marin County and San Jose to feast here. Parking can be a problem, but it's worth the search. The cryptic menu comes with clear translations, and you can have a dining experience for $5–$10. Open for lunch and dinner daily (closed 3–5 P.M.); 668–5888. AE/MC/V.

New Ocean, 239 Clement (668–1688), has you pick your fish while it's still swimming and then turns it into a remarkable lunch or dinner. One of the lobster dishes is cooked with ginger and onions, and a steamed whole crab comes with plum sauce. They also have clay-pot specials as part of what is basically Cantonese cuisine. The ambience is zippy; the English is limited, but the food is some of the best in town. The original **Oceans** at 726 Clement (221–3351) also is recommended, as much for the artistic presentation of the food as for its flavor. Both are open for lunch and dinner daily. AE/MC/V.

For a first venture beyond chow mein, **The Fountain Court Restaurant,** 354 Clement at Fifth (668–1100), is safe territory. Crisply modern, with a cream and turquoise decor, its extensive menu features Shanghai cuisine and has both pictures and English translations. Open daily for lunch and dinner. AE/DC/MC/V.

If Chinese doesn't appeal, **Cheers,** 127 Clement (387–6966), is a good alternative. This cheerful European-style café and espresso bar is a light and contemporary setting in which to wolf down pizzas, pastas, sandwiches, and salads. MC/V.

Another good short stop is the **Toy Boat Dessert Café,** 401 Clement (751–7505). San Francisco's prize-winning Double Rainbow ice cream is the big draw, along with pastries, espressos, and a mélange of mechanical tin toys (for sale).

Shopping

All of San Francisco's shopping is fun, but a few places stand out in almost all districts. Downtown, the **Galleria at Crocker Center** is setting the pace. Under its avant-garde arched skylight are 50 sophisticated, almost affordable shops on three levels, a lineal architectural descendant of the famous Galleria Vittorio Emmanuelle in Milan. This covered pedestrian way links Post and Sutter in mid-block between Montgomery and Kearney, and the chimes you hear on the hour throughout this part of downtown come from handsome clocks at both entrances. The *Polo/Ralph Lauren* store has his largest Home Collection in America, and designer fashions are featured at *New Man* (French); *Gianni Versace* (Italian); *Marimekko* (Finnish); and *Rodier Paris* (French). The best of American fashion reigns at *Peck & Peck, Casual Corner,* and *Laura Caspari.* Tiny ladies love *Especially Petites,* and *Arlequin* has unusual toys and clothes for children. *Japonesque* deals in the arts, crafts, and antiquities of Nippon.

Other specialty shops will tempt you with Godiva chocolates, unusual high-tech gifts and adult toys, custom-designed jewelry, and natural cosmetics. If you tire, there are numerous eateries, including *Phoebe's Entertainment Parlour,* where you can catch the soaps on big-screen TV. Better yet, grab a sandwich and picnic on the roof garden.

Maiden Lane is also fun to shop. The *Circle Gallery* at No. 140 shows the latest in art in a building designed by Frank Lloyd Wright. *Orvis* (No. 166) is outstanding for sporting goods and athletic clothing.

The north side of the 200–700 blocks of **Sutter Street** has become choice shopping of late, with fashionable clothing from *Jeanne Marc* (No. 262); frilly undies from *Victoria's Secret* (No. 395); fabrics and home accessories imported from Provence at *Pierre Deux* (No. 532); and *Therien & Co.* (No. 534) has the best of contemporary accessories scattered around on 17th- and 18th- century museum-quality furniture. The gourmet cookware and kitchen accessories at *Williams Sonoma* (No. 576) are famous among good cooks across America. The selection here is far more extensive than their catalog. *Australia Fair* (No. 700) sells giant rocking rams for children, plus all manner of goodies from down under, bush hats to stuffed koalas.

The south side of Sutter in this same area is art-gallery and antique-shop row. If you are feeling like an antique yourself, *LaBelle* (No. 575; 433–7644) can rejuvenate you from head to toe (ladies only). A large beauty parlor offering massages and facials (but not hairdressing), LaBelle also sells clothing. Further out, the 1100–1400 blocks focus on Oriental rugs.

The big news for fall 1988 is the opening of the new *Nordstrom's* in the 800 block of Market Street, opposite the cablecar terminus at Powell. A circular escalator carries shoppers up through the mall to the department store on the upper level.

San Francisco is also the hub of a major wholesale fashion and rag trade, and you can shop the sample and overrun racks at *Esprit* (821–2000) and *Six Sixty Center* (660 Third). To access other off-price firms, make an advance reservation with *Shopper Stopper* (707–829–1597). For a modest fee (about

$20), their color consultant guides will ferry you to at least six major outlets. Another specialty firm, *Showplace Tours* (558–8687), offers two-hour looks behind the scenes of Showplace Square, multiple buildings that make up the city's largest decorator district. Special arrangements allow you to buy antiques, furniture, home accessories, etc., from stores that normally sell "to the trade only."

If you love fine fabrics and sewing, don't miss *Britex,* 146 Geary. Fine yard goods from throughout the world are stacked floor to ceiling on four floors. You can sign up for their Britex-By-Mail personalized swatch service.

Want a pet robot or Swedish exercise bike? How about a computer card shark or a pocket TV? These and other electronic exotica are the focus of *The Sharper Image,* 532 Market, and also at Davis and Broadway. The quad towers of nearby **Embarcadero Center** have other enticements. In EC One, try *Little Daisy* (street and lobby levels) for outstanding dressy separates for women, and *Bentley's* (lobby level) for a kaleidoscope of accessories. *Outdoorsman of Lake Tahoe* and *Ingear* (lobby and podium levels) are repositories of outstanding sporting equipment and clothing from around the world. Three EC has a corner on female fashion, with *Ann Taylor* and *Le Beau Monde* stores. The latter shows the best of local designers.

EC Four is a cornucopia of special places. *The Nature Company* (street level) helps people enjoy nature without exploring it. You'll find inexpensive indoor/outdoor thermometers and bird feeders here, as well as animal figures in many media, books, globes, and handsome home accessories made from natural materials. Occasionally, there's a working artist tucked amid the displays—have a look. The Lalique and Baccarat crystal displays at *Pavillion de Paris* (street level) are dazzling—it's fun to see what rich people can afford!

EC Five has **The Magic If,** a fantasy of soft sculpture, and they'll do a caricature from a photograph, so come prepared. **Lotus** (parkway level) specializes in moderately priced earrings, many by San Francisco artists.

Good shopping is found in Pacific Heights, specifically near the intersection of Fillmore and Union. Some very special stops include *Shiota,* 3131 Fillmore, one of the best places in town for Japanese art and porcelains; *Oggetti,* 1846 Union, for the most elite of fine papers and stationery; and *Enchanted Crystal,* a fantasy of sparkling jewelry, decorative art, crystal, and art glass. *Fabulous Things,* 1974 Union, more homespun but just as delightful, is the top antique-quilt store in America. This is also a folk-art gallery, with whimsical wooden pieces displayed on an outstanding collection of antique Scandinavian and Irish furniture.

New and Old Estates, 2181–A Union, has estate jewelry, crystal, silver, and accessories at affordable prices but irregular hours. If the "open" sign is up, don't miss it.

Sacramento Street has its own rewards, as new retail shops open nearly every month. Among the best of the "old-timers" are *Bill Pearson Primitive Art,* 3499 Sacramento, specializing in pre-Columbian, Oceanic, African, and Northwestern antiques and art objects. Near the other end of the block is the *Unicef Store,* which is filled with unusual and inexpensive gifts and jewelry, some of which is ideal for children.

Ghirardelli Square, The Cannery, and Pier 39 all have outstanding shops, but you'll find those on your own!

Dining

Wander the city's many restaurant rows. Clement (Cle-
ment) Street in the Richmond District is happy hunting
ground—more than 80 eateries in less than a mile. Neighboring Geary Boulevard has even more, so if Clement fails you,
move one block south for fresh options. The Sunset District's
relatively low rents are attracting new restaurants—try No-
riega and Irving streets or along Ninth Avenue. Union and
Sacramento streets in Pacific Heights and the shopping zones
of Fisherman's Wharf are other good choices, and more trendy watering holes are sure to open in the hot Jackson Square-
Levi Plaza zone. Tiny cubbyholes and basements along Sutter, Bush, and Post in the upper Union Square area are turning into dining finds almost by the week. You'll probably beat
the guidebook writers to something new and marvelous within blocks of your hotel.

A few guidelines: Even if a restaurant is open until 3 or 4 A.M., the bar must close by 2 A.M. Tipping generally is 15 percent of the pretax amount.

PICNICS

No dining in San Francisco is more enjoyable than a fine picnic. From the Embarcadero to Golden Gate Park, Union Square to the Palace of Fine Arts, this is an alfresco town. Most of the city's delicatessens will pack a sandwich or salad to go, so let's focus on those specialty businesses that go one or two steps further. In addition to City Picnic and Napper's Too (discussed in the Downtown chapter), the following pack a memorable hamper.

Vivande, 2125 Fillmore in lower Pacific Heights, is out of the way but worth the search. In addition to a well-stocked deli-counter that's usually three deep in customers, this is a 40-seat cafe open daily. Almost everything is made on the premises, and much of it is unique to Vivande. The Torta Milanese is a layered affair of egg, cheese, tomato, spinach, ham, and peppers that's sold by the thick slice. The chicken Mattone is cooked Sicilian-style, highly seasoned and then grilled under a brick. Ever had an eggplant and provolone sandwich? Smoked chicken salad? Sausage with fennel? This is the place. With some advance notice (two hours or more; 346–4430), they'll design a picnic to your taste and toss in forks, plates, and napkins. Italian sodas and a broad selection of beers and wines are chilled and ready to depart on your feast. AE/CB/DC/MC/V.

Ever munched on a designer sandwich? No? A picnic from **Picnix** will fill this void in your food experience. How about a Kate Hepburn (chicken breast, hickory bacon, swiss, lettuce, tomato) or a Grace Kelly (chicken breast, avocado, hickory bacon, watercress, on cottage-cheese dill bread)? Then come your just desserts—chocolate fudge or lemon-buttermilk cake. Box lunches start at $7; a split of wine is extra, but advice on the best picnic spots is free. Picnix is now also a bistro, serving soups, salads, sandwiches, and quiche at lunch. Closed Sunday. No credit cards. 423 Presidio, between California and Sacramento (922–4900).

If hunger strikes while you are in the Fisherman's Wharf area, why not picnic in the Aquatic Park? You'll find all the fixings at **Picnic,** a gourmet deli on the main floor of the Cannery (775–3434). They'll assemble a lunch to go while you shop the neighboring kiosks. One is a wine cellar with 526 different beers. Open daily. AE/MC/V.

LITE BITES

The dual snack spots, **Max's Citicourt Cafe** and **Max's at the Conservatory,** both at One Sansome in the Financial District, can satisfy whatever midday cravings you might have. The first has more complete meals; the second is great for sandwiches and picnic fixings. The café is open weekdays for lunch and dinner; the conservatory offers breakfast things as well. Closed on weekends (362–MAXS). AE/MC/V.

Want dim sum to go? Try **The Fook Restaurant,** 332 Clement (668–8070). A single $1.44 order has 3–4 dumplings filled with beef, shrimp, or pork—you choose from big steamers. Open from 9 A.M. to midnight daily. AE/MC/V.

It's easy to whip right by **Teddy's at the Cartwright,** but then you would miss the turkey tango salad, the memorable quiche, and other breakfast and luncheon specials. Open daily, 7 A.M. to 4 P.M. Mr. Teddy also serves a scrumptious tea from 2 to 4 P.M. Ask about his dieter's specials. Reservations advised (524 Sutter; 956–0493). AE/MC/V.

SF's pizza lovers have found a pocket-sized pizza parlor called **Vicolo,** 201 Ivy at Franklin (863–2382), behind the Hayes Street Grill. In addition to serving the ultimate wedge, they have Italian side salads and ice cream; it's a snacking good place. Now also at Ghiradelli Square. Open daily, lunch till late. No credit cards.

BREAKFAST

Getting a good breakfast often can be the challenge of a trip. In addition to Teddy's in the Lite Bites section, the Buena Vista in the Northern Waterfront section, and Campton Place in the American/Regional section, the following win honors:

Smack in the middle of downtown, half a block from Union Square, **Sears** has a devoted clientele, as much for its fresh fruits in season as for its perfectly done eggs and crisp hash brown potatoes. There is an in-house bakery, so the coffee cake is still warm from the oven, and the Swedish pancakes with maple syrup are worth even a trip across town. No credit cards, no dinners, no alcoholic beverages. Open from 7 A.M. to 2:30 P.M., Wednesday through Sunday. (439 Powell, near Bush; 986–1160.)

Mama's, on Washington Square in North Beach (362–6421), serves breakfast from 7:30 A.M. to 3 P.M. weekdays, until 4 P.M. weekends. Try the French toast with your choice of breads and fresh fruit topping, or one of the imaginative omelets. No credit cards. Mama's newest venture, also called **Mama's,** serves the same goodies as well as a full menu nearly around the clock at 398 Geary (downtown as Mason; 788–1004). AE/DC/MC/V.

VERY SAN FRANCISCO

Hopefully, you've already sampled Tadich's, Sam's Grill, and John's Grill, discussed in the Downtown chapter. Here are two more very special SF treats:

If you are feeling adventurous, make reservations at the highly rated **California Culinary Academy,** freshly ensconced in new digs at 265 Polk, at Turk (771–3500). You may be served by one of the next wonders of the cooking world or by one destined for the doggie diner. Student chefs prepare and serve meals that range from unremarkable to outstanding, depending on the brilliance of the teaching chef overseeing them all. You can control the odds to some degree by choosing carefully among the eight entrées. The desserts always are good bets. Lunch seatings are at noon and 1 P.M., dinner seatings at 6 and 7:30 P.M. Open weekdays only; prices are moderate. A full-service bar has been added, plus a no-reservation à la carte service upstairs at lunch, nice for eating light at the last minute. Free tours of the academy are given weekdays at 3 P.M. AE/DC/MC/V.

The **Garden Court of the Sheraton Palace Hotel** has been a San Francisco institution for generations. An elegant, glass-domed ballroom with marble pillars and glittering chandeliers, this is the place for a dress-up brunch. Open for breakfast and lunch weekdays; Sunday brunch with harpist and dinner buffet with string quartet. (639 Market St. at California; 392–8600.) AE/CB/DC/MC/V.

SEAFOOD

Fresh fish, in infinite variety and dress, is the menu mainstay of almost every restaurant in town, and oyster bars are cropping up in some surprising places. Again, Sam's and Tadich's are good choices, but, in general, Fisherman's Wharf is not.

The **Hayes Street Grill** in Civic Center features fresh fish daily on its blackboard menu, either grilled over mesquite charcoal or in dishes like California fish stew or clams Provençale. You'll also find smoked chicken or warm quail salad here, along with tasty sausages made on-site and a choice selection of grilled meats. There's also a full bar with the best California wine list in the city. Five wines are selected weekly to be available by the glass ($2.25–$4). One of the pioneers in the renaissance of Hayes Street, this clean-lined restaurant is a favorite of businessmen, performers, and the theater crowd. In evenings you'll see everything from evening gowns and tuxes to designer jeans. There's a $7.50 minimum charge per person, $10 minimum on Visa or MasterCard charges. Open weekdays for lunch, Monday through Saturday for dinner. Reservations advised at night. (320 Hayes St., corner of Franklin; 863–5545.)

Scott's Seafood Grill and Bar is a good place for a hot crab-cake sandwich, fisherman's stew, grilled salmon, or almost anything else that swims in the sea. Crowds are the rule at the original Lombard location. You'll have better luck getting a table at their Embarcadero Three dining room. The atmosphere is casual, the prices are moderate, and the menu's all fish. (2400 Lombard at Scott; 563–8988. Embarcadero Three, podium level; 981–0622.) Lunch and dinner daily. AE/CB/DC/MC/V.

The "air-cooled" dining room of the **Elite Cafe** is a page from the Art Deco '30s with its private booths, long bar with oak swivel chairs, and marble-topped oyster bar. A Cajun cook reigns, so expect blackened redfish and shrimp *étouffée* amid the Maryland crab, oysters, and inventive beef, pork, and chicken. Open daily for dinner, brunch, too, on Sunday. No reservations. (2049 Fillmore; 346–8668.) AE/MC/V.

AMERICAN/REGIONAL

If you've already sampled Square One and Stars (Downtown chapter), you can continue your quest for the best at the following.

Touches of the Orient, a smidgeon of California flair, a stir or two of nouvelle, and a soupçon of Français—at **Silks,** master chef Howard Bulka draws on all the food disciplines to create new dishes from the best of the classics. Don't come here unless you can linger. Just absorbing the suggested tastes and nuances of the menu is a pleasure. Will it be the Caribbean shrimp sided with potato fritters and mango chutney? Perhaps the crispy duck *confit* served in Calvados cream? You'll even be tempted to settle for three of the appetizers and then splurge on an equal number of desserts. Whatever you choose, you'll never forget the pleasures of the food. Breakfast and dinner Monday through Saturday, lunch on weekdays, brunch on Sunday. Reservations essential. (222 Sansome, in the Mandarin Oriental Hotel; 885–0999.) AE/CB/DC/MC/V.

What could be more American than a great piece of beef? If steak or prime rib sounds just right, call for a table at **Harris'.** Not only is the best of beef aged properly in the foyer refrigerator cases, it's cooked to perfection and served in a room highlighted by a Barnaby Conrad mural depicting the Harris Ranch in the Kings River Canyon. Lunch weekdays, dinner nightly; jackets for men required. (2100 Van Ness; 673–1888.) AE/MC/V.

One of the kickiest eateries in town, **Rosalie's,** at 1415 Van Ness, has a growing reputation for inventive Southwestern food, thanks to its young lady chef, Rick O'Connell. Only here: loin of pork smoked on-site and roasted in a brown sugar/bourbon sauce and then served with bananas fried in beer batter and with a spicy black bean cake. And you thought barbecue was just barbecue! Nor can you go wrong with either the shellfish pan-roast or the nightly specials. The room itself is a show. Near the front it is all steel gray and white—metal banana palms with mirrored trunks, galvanized steel table tops, etc.—and then color begins to spice up the scene as you move to the back of the space. Open for lunch and dinner daily; reservations advised (928–7188). AE/CB/DC/MC/V.

FRENCH

Another top contender for the "Best Restaurant in SF" award is **Fleur de Lys,** 777 Sutter (673–7779). The draped setting is luscious and intimate, and the food goes far beyond either the classic or bourgeois dishes of France. Chef Hubert Keller utilizes the west coast's bounty of fresh fish, vegetables, and fruit in unusual ways—bring your appetite. Dinner Monday through Saturday. AE/CB/DC/MC/V.

Le Castel in lower Pacific Heights also is elegant with tasty offerings, its à la carte menu written in French with English translations in the margin. Alsatian dishes are favorites here, and the food is tasty, inventive, and nouvelle. There's a dressy pink-and-maroon drawing-room atmosphere here, plus a semi-celebrity clientele. Dinner only, Monday through Saturday; reservations essential. (3235 Sacramento St., between Presidio and Lyon; 921–7115.) AE/DC/MC/V.

Le Central is another celebrity hangout, particularly for lunch. The cassoulet and sauerkraut pots have been brewing on the stove of this unpretentious brasserie since it opened over a decade ago, the most flavorful in town. The French country menu is almost encyclopedic, and new lighter offerings are making headway here. The windows of the restaurant section roll back on nice days, giving the feel of an open-air café. Lunch on weekdays, dinner Monday through Saturday. (453 Bush St.; 391–2233.) AE/MC/V.

The best of the day's fresh fish, meats, and vegetables appear on the blackboard menu of **Rue Lepic,** another creative endeavor of Gerardo Boccara of the Nob Hill Café (discussed in the Downtown chapter). A little larger, with a more sophisticated Art Deco decor, this French/Japanese grill is a growing neighborhood favorite among Nob Hill's charge-card clientele. Dinner nightly. (900 Pine St.; 474–6070.) MC/V.

Unusual interpretations of the classic bourgeois cuisine of France are **Zola's** long suit. If you love French food in all its forms, come here. Chef Catherine Patsios and partner Larry Bain have created one gem of a dining experience. The food is inventive and comes as art-on-the-plate in ample, if not lavish, amounts. Larry seats you and explains the menu and wines to be considered, and then begins a dinner like none other in the city. Save room for two desserts, so you won't miss the bread pudding with fresh fruit sauce (unlike any Mom ever made) or the homemade sorbets. A dinner (without wine) for one will cost under $20. Open Tuesday through Saturday for dinner; reservations essential. (1722 Sacramento St.; 775–3311.) AE/DC/MV/V.

CONTINENTAL

For romantic dining, few places match **Café Mozart.** The two small Viennese-style dining rooms are set with three or four tables for two, and it's very much a candlelight-and-roses atmosphere. Austrian sheers and heavy velvet drapes keep the world away, crystal chandeliers help you read the menu, and Mozart's musical notes hang in the air. The expensive ($43) but inventive prix fixe dinner changes constantly but usually offers superbly flavored cream and clear soups, two cold and three hot appetizers, several entrees, and two other courses. The aromas coming from the open kitchen are divine. House specials change from season to season, but they may include salmon cooked in parchment, venison, and tournedos with green peppercorn sauce. The wine list is carefully chosen, and should you want just a glass, the selected vintage is uncorked, poured, and left at your table on the honor system. Open daily except Sunday for dinner until 10 P.M., and reservations are recommended. (708 Bush St.; 391–8480.) MC/V.

The French Continental menu is extensive at the elegant **Carnelian Room** on top of the Bank of America building, but it's always second banana to the panoramic view of the city. Cocktails begin at 3 P.M. weekdays, 4 P.M. Saturdays. Dinners, from 6–10:30 P.M. nightly, and Sunday brunch are highly recommended. This is a grand place for a sunset dinner and drink or a tag-of-the-evening nightcap. Reservations are advised. (555 California St.; 433–7500.) AE/CB/DC/MC/V.

The richly flavored foods of Czechoslovakia, Austria, and Hungary are the specialties of **Heart of Europe,** an immaculate basement bistro find in the upper Union Square zone. Cooked up by recent Czech immigrant Joseph Erlec, the moderately priced dinner ranges from a traditional Hungarian goulash and a habit-forming potato pancake sandwich to daily specials. Dinners include salad and fresh vegetables and your choice of eight or nine entrees. Beer buffs note: they import Dortmunder Kronen beer (on tap) and Pilsner Urquell, the oldest beer in the world. They also have hard-to-get Czech and German liquors. Reservations are recommended, particularly for Friday and Saturday nights when there's live entertainment. Lunch weekdays, dinner nightly. The bar is open until 2 A.M. (685 Sutter; 441–5678.) AE/MC/V.

If a decor could be described as contemporary Victorian, **Ivy's Restaurant and Bar** would be exhibit A. This classy ivy/palm establishment is one of the new signs of the good life in the Civic Center locale, one block from both the symphony hall and opera house. The California-style menu has Continental overtones and changes daily, and the richly colored rooms are lined with photos of music and ballet greats. Lunch and dinner served daily; reservations are suggested. (398 Hayes St.; 626–3930.) AE/MC/V.

Billed as Italian, **Angelino's** offers a Continental menu with numerous seafood dishes. Its growing reputation, however, is for its fresh pasta—folks grow rapturous about the seafood linguine. Squeaky clean with napery and fresh flowers on the tables, it's a good choice for lunch or dinner in Sausalito. Open daily. (621 Bridgeway; 331–5225.) AE/MC/V.

For elegant dining in Sausalito, consider **Ondine,** with its waterfront location and twinkling view at night. Specialties include rack of lamb Belvedere, fresh foie gras, salmon au Champagne, and an impressive trio of dessert soufflés. The atmosphere, cuisine, and tab are *très* haute, so dress for the occasion. Lunch and dinner served daily; reservations advised. (558 Bridgeway—with Horizons—332–0791, or 982–1740 from SF.) AE/CB/DC/MC/V.

There are several good reasons to compete for a table at **Faz,** a find at 132 Bush in the financial district. Chef/owner Fazol Poursohi personally buys the best produce from local farms, the meats and fish are smoked in house, and the afford-able menu is the same for lunch and dinner, Monday through Friday (362–4484). AE/CB/DC/MC/V.

Looking for an inexpensive lunch or dinner in pricey down-town? Head for the **Post Street Bar and Café.** Clean of line and inventive of kitchen, this light, bright contemporary res-taurant has earned its stars in a tough restaurant town. The daily chef specials are the reason for a high repeat business. Open for lunch weekdays, dinner Tuesday through Saturday. (632 Post St.; 928–2080.) AE/MC/V.

Masa's is a tough reservation to get on the spur of the mo-ment. If you are intent on eating here, make your trip plans around table availability. The food is extraordinary and *très* nouvelle, the legacy of the late Masa Kobayashi as enlarged upon (with success) by current chef Julian Serrano. The handsome room and service will make you feel like a million-aire—and you'll wish you were one when you get the check! (648 Bush in the Hotel Vintage Court; 989–7154.) AE/DC/MC/V.

While dining at **The Palm** isn't an only-in-San-Francisco experience—there are clones in several other cities, plus the well-established original in New York—it is one of the most heady experiences in town. There's a vitality here unequalled at any other eatery, a sense of being in on SF's action. The cartoon-festooned walls are fun, the menu extensive, the steaks superb, the Nova Scotia lobsters gigantic, and the cheesecake imported from NYC. What more could you want? Well, there's the huge pimiento and anchovies salad or the Roquefort and vinaigrette salad dressing to think about. Open for lunch and dinner, Monday through Saturday. (586 Bush; 981–1222.) AE/CB/DC/MC/V.

ASIAN

Pot Sticker is an inexpensive but tasty solution to the "where to snack in Chinatown" dilemma, a small place with brick walls and plants and a minimum of Chinese gewgaws. In fact, the ethnically neutral atmosphere could fool you into thinking it was a hamburger or pizza joint. Not by a long shot. The house specialty is pot stickers, little pan-fried dumplings stuffed with seasoned meat or vegetables. The

menu also has some interesting Szechuan and Mandarin offerings, like orange spareribs. In all, this is a good place for
that first venture beyond egg rolls and chow mein. Next door
and upstairs is a Chinese temple where visitors usually are
welcome. Burn some incense for good joss. Ask your waiter
or the cashier for special directions. Open daily from 11:30
A.M. to 4 P.M.; dinner from 4:30–9:30 P.M. (150 Waverly Place;
397–9985.) AE/MC/V.

Mai's Vietnamese at its original location on Clement is a
basic beige and formica, family-run, no-nonsense sort of
place. The newer, flossier location on Union serves the same
great food in more pleasant surroundings, with some tables
outside in front so you can watch the passing human parade.
You usually can have your pick of tables at the Union Street
location. The food at both is cooked only when ordered and
is some of the best Vietnamese in town. The spicy prawns,
though not as hot as the Indonesian or Thai versions, will
perk up your palate, and the sautéed beef in coconut sauce
is another hands-down favorite. Imperial rolls and the shrimp
balls also are recommended. Open weekdays for lunch, nightly for dinner. (316 Clement St.; 221–3046; or 1838 Union;
921–2861.) AE/MC/V.

For Japanese food, try **Yoshida-Ya,** off Union Street in Pacific Heights. They have sushi, but no sushi bar. Instead, the
house specialty is yakitori—bamboo skewers of charcoal-
grilled beef, chicken, or fish served with a spicy sauce. Downstairs has a bar and eating area; upstairs is the more traditional Japanese dining room with lacquered tables above seating
pits. Open for lunch on weekends, dinner nightly. (2909 Webster, off Union; 346–3431.) AE/CB/DC/MC/V.

Japan Center is filled with restaurants. Peruse them all, and
then settle on one or two for their specialties. Suggested are
Mitoya and **Fuki-Ya** for *robata-yaki.* These are skewers load-
ed with your choice from the array of food displayed—fish,
vegetables, chicken, beef—and then grilled before you on a
hibachi. **Mifune** and **Sapporo-Ya** are grand for Japanese noodles—slurping is considered a compliment to the chef—and
Isobune is a novel place for sushi; you'll see why.

Other good choices include Grand Palace and Yank Sing
for dim sum, Sam Wo for noodles and *jook,* and Imperial Palace for everything else. All are discussed fully in the China-
town/North Beach chapter. The Mandarin (Northern Wa-

terfront chapter) is outstanding, as are Angkor Wat and
Ocean/New Ocean, discussed in the Golden Gate Park chapter.

ITALIAN

In addition to Caffe Quadro and Ciao (Downtown chapter), Magic Flute (Sacramento Street), and the eateries already listed in the North Beach chapter, the following places know their pastas.

Modesto Lanzone's is a hands-down favorite for the best of Italian food. Their Opera Plaza location (601 Van Ness Ave.) is decorated with Lanzone's personal collection of modern art, a handsome foil for outstanding works, primarily by major Italian and Northern California artists. If you restrain yourself when the appetizer cart comes around—you can select one or all of the six to eight offerings—try the Panzoti di Recco (a fresh pasta stuffed with ricotta cheese and walnut sauce) or the Bauletto di Vitello Romana (sliced veal folded with prosciutto and mushrooms). The zabaglione is incredible—a light mix of eggs, lemon, vanilla, and Marsala. The ambience is comfortably dressy, and the à la carte menu items are in the moderate range. Open for lunch on weekdays, dinner Monday through Saturday. Reservations strongly advised. Note: Unless the Performing Arts Center is swinging, on-street parking usually is relatively easy to find in the Opera Plaza area. (928–0400). AE/CB/DC/MC/V.

Two North Beach restaurants approach Italian food from different angles. **Capp's Corner** is one of the last of its kind, the inexpensive family-style place where the minestrone arrives at your table in a giant tureen. Gourmet it isn't, honest and filling it is. The place is always full and always fun. Family photos are on the walls amid signed shots of local fighters, movie stars, and sports figures, the Rogue's Gallery of a corner trattoria that made good. Reservations suggested. Open Tuesday through Friday for lunch, nightly for dinner. (1600 Powell at Green; 989–2589.) MC/V.

Caffe Sport isn't a restaurant, it's a psychedelic experience that happens to serve food. This crazy hole-in-the-wall establishment has been the folk-art canvas of Sicilian owner and chef Toni La Tona for 18 years. Descriptions cannot do it justice, so drop in for at least a beer. The food is good, but fair warning: He claims to use a hundred pounds of garlic every five days in creating his various sauces. No credit cards are honored. Open for lunch and dinner (till late), Tuesday through Saturday. (574 Green; 981–1251.)

Cafés and
Nightlife

Where to go at night in San Francisco depends upon what you enjoy. For people-watching and general atmosphere, Enrico's Sidewalk Café on Broadway is one of the best. When there's a lull in the action, you can wander up Columbus to Café Puccini or Caffe Roma, or join the late-night crowds at Café Trieste. All are covered in the North Beach section.

Comedy clubs always have been one of the city's hallmarks—Phyllis Diller, Mort Sahl, and Woody Allen were headliners here in their early careers—and you'll find a new crop of laugh-makers at various places around town. **The Punch Line,** 444-A Battery St. (397-7573), is a good place to start. A trim restaurant and bar favored by the young professional crowd, it features local and national comedians Tuesday through Sunday nights. Call for times and headliners. Tickets range from $3 to $8, and there's a two-drink minimum.

The Last Day Saloon is lively at 406 Clement (387–6343). Drop in for dancing and to catch one of the blues, rock, or Motown acts. Recent shows have featured Maria Muldaur, Dr. John of Louisiana rhythm-and-blues fame, and Mary Wells, the queen of Motown. Cover ranges from $2 to $12, depending on the type of show, and no credit cards are accepted. Also, there's a one-drink ($2–$3.50) minimum per set. Open nightly until 2 A.M.

Comedians have to start somewhere, and for Robin Williams it was **The Holy City Zoo,** 408 Clement in the Richmond district (386–4242). To hear the best and worst of SF's homegrown talent, catch Open Mike on Sunday and Tuesday nights. Pros headline throughout the week. Call for fees and playbill. **Cobb's Comedy Club,** 2801 Leavenworth (at The Cannery; 928–4320), headlines pros nightly. No credit cards accepted. Cover charges at both clubs range from about $2 to $12, and two-drink minimums apply.

You'll also find comedy acts at **The Great American Music Hall,** 859 O'Farrell (885–0750), interspersed with big names in jazz, folk, rock, and country music. Recent headliners have ranged from B.B. King to the Zazu Pitts Memorial Orchestra. Show dates, times, and cover charges vary, so call before you go. No credit cards or reservations, but you can get tickets in advance through BASS outlets (762–BASS or 800–225–2277). Call the club for recorded information and times of current shows. Street caution is advised in this neighborhood at night.

Bearing little resemblance to its Laredo namesake and tucked at the end of an alley near Moscone Center, the **Cadillac Bar** still draws crowds. The restaurant's specials are cabrito and Polla al Mesquite, and the bar makes a big thing out of sangria and margaritas. Overall, the atmosphere is southwestern/Meheecano, down to the long, sombrero-topped bar. The large warehouse-style room usually is filled with upwardly mobile types, for this is the place to meet after work. Mariachis play, ceiling fans whir, and it's good fun. Lunch served weekdays, dinner Monday through Saturday; no reservations. (1 Holland Court, off Howard between 4th and 5th Sts.; 543–8226.) AE/MC/V.

Kimball's, 300 Grove St., at Franklin in Civic Center (861–5555), is basically a restaurant but also is one of the best of the many jazz clubs in town Wednesday through Saturday nights. Schedules are published monthly of who plays when, and cover charges range from $2 to $12.50, depending on whether the likes of Stan Getz or a new local group is in the spotlight. Also, there's a two-drink minimum. AE/MC/V.

Are you hot to do the twist, the hokeypokey, or the hula hoop? If so, there are two crazy discos you shouldn't miss. **Rockin Robins,** at 1840 Haight (near Golden Gate Park), swings with the music of the '50s and '60s from noon to 2 A.M. daily (221–1960). The DJ sits in part of an old car suspended from the ceiling, and other "car-tifacts" jut from the walls. There's also large-screen satellite TV for those quiet moments of recuperation. Across town, **Jukebox Saturday Night** follows a similar game plan at 650 Howard, part of the South-of-Market fun (495–JUKE). Again, the music is Motown of the '50s and '60s, and the DJ sits in what was the front of a '57 Chevy in another life. The lunch menu runs to hamburgers, the soda fountain features Double Rainbow ice cream, and nine TV screens are scattered around the room. Open from 11 A.M. to 2 A.M. daily.

Two cabarets downtown can be counted on for an evening's entertainment. With its stained-glass ceiling and cushy chairs, **The Plush Room** is a pleasure, with live performances by such as Michael Feinstein, Margaret Whiting, and Julie Wilson nightly, except Monday. Call for prices and details (940 Sutter, off the lobby of the York Hotel; 885–6800). **City Cabaret,** 401 Mason at Geary (441–RSVP), has jazz, comedy, music, or variety shows nightly, featuring the likes of Barbara Cook and Nanette Fabray. Cover ranges from $5–$20, and there is no drink requirement.

"Beach Blanket Babylon," has been playing for over a decade at **Club Fugazi** (678 Green St. in North Beach). A wild mix of song, dance, zany costumes, and towering headgear, this became the longest running musical review in theater history in July 1984, surpassing even the Ziegfeld Follies. Tickets range from $12.50 to $20, depending on time of day of performance, and can be ordered up to two months in advance, so don't delay. Seating is cabaret-style, and drinks (wine, beer, champagne, soft drinks) start at $1.50 (421–4222). MC/V.

Gay bars are scattered around town, the majority in the Castro district and along Polk Street. Not all welcome straights, but if you want to make that scene, try **The Stud,** 399 Ninth St.; **Café San Marcos,** 2367 Market; or **Trocadero Transfer,** 520 Fourth St.

HOTEL HIGHLIGHTS

Major headliners like Tony Bennett, Nancy Wilson, Bernadette Peters, and Sergio Mendes/Brazil '88 keep the **Fairmont Hotel's Venetian Room** perennially on top of the supper-club heap. Dinners range from $20 to $26, and the shows are an additional $17–$25, with dancing to Dick Bright's Orchestra tossed in to sweeten the pot. Showtimes are 9:30 P.M. on Sunday, Tuesday, Wednesday, and Thursday; 9 and 11 P.M. on Friday and Saturday. Reservations are a must (772–5163 or 772–5000). The Venetian Room is included on some of the organized nightclub tours at considerable savings. Check with the San Francisco Convention and Visitors Bureau for particulars. Also fun: Gershwin, jazz, and swing music in the Fairmont's **New Orleans Room** Tuesday through Saturday.

Other San Francisco hotels swing after dark. You can hear jazz piano at the **One Up Lounge** atop the Hyatt-Union Square, or relax at **L'Etoile's Lounge** in the Huntington Hotel, where Peter Mintum masters the keyboard. The **Other Trellis** at the Hyatt Regency at Embarcadero Center swings with Dixieland on Saturday from 3 to 8 P.M. and with show tunes by Jimmy Diamond on Sunday from 4 to 8 P.M. The adjacent **Market Place Restaurant** has live music daily from late afternoon on.

If you feel like dancing, try the **Starlite Roof** of the Sir Francis Drake Hotel, Powell and Sutter (392–7755). Trios play dance music here from 9 P.M. to 1 A.M. (mostly swing), and although there is no cover charge, there is a one-drink minimum.

The hottest disco in town is **OZ,** a fantasyland for adults on the 32nd floor of the Westin St. Francis on Union Square. Enjoyment of the panoramic view begins with sunset cocktails at 4:30 P.M. daily (no cover), and music engineered by Juliana's of London plays from 9:30 P.M. to 2 A.M., Sunday through Thursday, and until 3 A.M. on Friday and Saturday (cover charge). This is a private-membership club, but if you are sober and well-dressed, they'll let you in to dance on the huge marble floor. Even though OZ holds more than 300 of SF's swankiest young crowd, best call for a reservation on Friday or Saturday night (397-7000).

A slightly more mature crowd prefers the oriental antique atmosphere of the St. Francis' **Compass Rose** off the lobby, where the Abe Battat trio plays favorite dance tunes nightly.

WITHOUT DRINKS

If your plans include a night at the theater, call 673-6440 for the playbill of the **American Conservatory Theatre.** Their basic October to May, 10-play season at the Geary Theatre (415 Geary St.) is supplemented by long-running shows during the summer months.

Greater Tuna runs in perpetuity at the Mason Street Theatre (668-TUNA), and you'll also find good shows at the **Waterfront Theatre** in Ghirardelli Square (885-2929) and at the **Zephyr Theatre** in the Civic Center (441-7787).

And for those spur of the moment plans, check with STBS for half-price tickets (433-STBS).

The famous **San Francisco International Film Festival** is the hottest ticket in town for ten days in March at the AMC Kabuki 8 Cinemas, 1881 Post (221-FILM). Get tickets and information through the BASS ticket centers scattered around town (762-2277 or 800-225-2277).

Tickets for the regular season of the **San Francisco Symphony** can be scarce, especially since the orchestra has moved into the handsome Louise M. Davies Symphony Hall. However, the traditional September–May season has been expanded with additional concerts in the summer and by guest appearances of major artists throughout the year. The Symphony also sponsors a Beethoven Festival in late June and a Mozart Festival in July. Your best bet is to call the Symphony Box Office and see what's available (431-5400).

The **San Francisco Opera's** season is September through mid-December, after which the stage of the Opera House belongs to the **San Francisco Ballet.** After a lavish production of *The Nutcracker* in December, the Ballet season runs through May. For tickets and information on the opera, call 864–3330; for the ballet, call 621–3838, 762–2277, or 800–225–2277.

San Francisco Performances also bring headliners to town October through May, with performances in Herbst Theatre of the War Memorial Veterans Building and Davies Symphony Hall. For information and tickets, call 626–6596.

Index

115

Fodor's Travel Guides

U.S. Guides

Alaska
American Cities
The American South
Arizona
Atlantic City & the
 New Jersey Shore
Boston
California
Cape Cod
Carolinas & the
 Georgia Coast
Chesapeake
Chicago
Colorado
Dallas & Fort Worth
Disney World & the
 Orlando Area

The Far West
Florida
Greater Miami,
 Fort Lauderdale,
 Palm Beach
Hawaii
Hawaii (Great Travel
 Values)
Houston & Galveston
I-10: California to
 Florida
I-55: Chicago to New
 Orleans
I-75: Michigan to
 Florida
I-80: San Francisco to
 New York

I-95: Maine to Miami
Las Vegas
Los Angeles, Orange
 County, Palm Springs
Maui
New England
New Mexico
New Orleans
New Orleans (Pocket
 Guide)
New York City
New York City (Pocket
 Guide)
New York State
Pacific North Coast
Philadelphia
Puerto Rico (Fun in)

Rockies
San Diego
San Francisco
San Francisco (Pocket
 Guide)
Texas
United States of
 America
Virgin Islands
 (U.S. & British)
Virginia
Waikiki
Washington, DC
Williamsburg,
 Jamestown &
 Yorktown

Foreign Guides

Acapulco
Amsterdam
Australia, New Zealand
 & the South Pacific
Austria
The Bahamas
The Bahamas (Pocket
 Guide)
Barbados (Fun in)
Beijing, Guangzhou &
 Shanghai
Belgium & Luxembourg
Bermuda
Brazil
Britain (Great Travel
 Values)
Canada
Canada (Great Travel
 Values)
Canada's Maritime
 Provinces
Cancún, Cozumel,
 Mérida, The
 Yucatán
Caribbean
Caribbean (Great
 Travel Values)

Central America
Copenhagen,
 Stockholm, Oslo,
 Helsinki, Reykjavik
Eastern Europe
Egypt
Europe
Europe (Budget)
Florence & Venice
France
France (Great Travel
 Values)
Germany
Germany (Great Travel
 Values)
Great Britain
Greece
Holland
Hong Kong & Macau
Hungary
India
Ireland
Israel
Italy
Italy (Great Travel
 Values)
Jamaica (Fun in)

Japan
Japan (Great Travel
 Values)
Jordan & the Holy Land
Kenya
Korea
Lisbon
Loire Valley
London
London (Pocket Guide)
London (Great Travel
 Values)
Madrid
Mexico
Mexico (Great Travel
 Values)
Mexico City & Acapulco
Mexico's Baja & Puerto
 Vallarta, Mazatlán,
 Manzanillo, Copper
 Canyon
Montreal
Munich
New Zealand
North Africa
Paris
Paris (Pocket Guide)

People's Republic of
 China
Portugal
Province of Quebec
Rio de Janeiro
The Riviera (Fun on)
Rome
St. Martin / St. Maarten
Scandinavia
Scotland
Singapore
South America
South Pacific
Southeast Asia
Soviet Union
Spain
Spain (Great Travel
 Values)
Sweden
Switzerland
Sydney
Tokyo
Toronto
Turkey
Vienna
Yugoslavia

Special-Interest Guides

Bed & Breakfast
Guide: North America
1936...On the
Continent

Royalty Watching
Selected Hotels of
Europe

Selected Resorts
and Hotels of the U.S.
Ski Resorts of North
America

Views to Dine by
around the World